Table of Contents

To the Teacher

Thank you for choosing *Take It Easy! Second Edition*. The Teacher's Manual for the second edition has been updated and includes Japanese translations of the Word Bank section. An additional section offers suggestions for how to vary and supplement the topics and activities.

Guide to Teaching Tips and Basic Teaching Plans

This guide is simple, and it looks at each section of a unit and offers suggestions for how to teach it. This guide does not look at each unit separately.

Before You Begin Teaching

Before beginning to use *Take It Easy! Second Edition*, the teacher needs to consider the following tips in order to make this textbook easier to teach and more beneficial to students.

1. **Consistently encourage the "Read, Look Up, Say'" technique.**
    In order to follow this, students must look at a conversation line, read as much as they can, and then look up and say it to their partners. By doing this, students can begin to memorize certain passages or phrases from the conversation examples instead of simply reading it in a flat tone. If the teacher constantly reminds students to follow this technique, students will naturally use it during their practice sessions.

2. **Make sure that students talk with everyone in class.**
    A communicative classroom will ensure that students talk to all classmates and not only with their friends or students who sit nearby. By talking to everyone in class, students will develop deeper communication skills and get to know everyone in class.

3. **Use pairs as often as possible but offer variation periodically by forming groups of three or four.**
    Pair work is highly suggested as it allows for the most conversation turns during activities.

4. **Keep track of students' speaking errors while monitoring speaking activities.**
    These can then be discussed orally or on the board with students.

5. **Establish a consistent homework pattern that will encourage students to study outside of class.**
    By following an expected pattern, students will understand that homework is useful for preparing for classes as it increases knowledge and skills.

Using Audio Scripts in Class

Using the audio scripts for the listening activities is highly recommended as it gives students other examples of the grammar or speaking point that is being studied. It is recommended that the teacher make copies available for students as paper handouts or digital PDFs. There are several possible approaches.

1. After taking up answers for a listening activity, have students take out their scripts and read them out loud with a partner. Use the "Read, Look Up, Say" technique.

2. Photocopy the audio script for any unit and do a cloze exercise. This can still be considered a listening activity.

3. Have students first read certain sections or conversations and prepare to retell or summarize the conversations to their partners.

4. Have students read the scripts as they listen. Then, have students answer the questions.

5. Look at the questions first. Then, have students listen and read, and underline the answers to the questions.

6. Use the scripts for shadowing, and have students listen and repeat what they have heard. Shadowing should be used to improve intonation, stress, and pronunciation.

Talking Naturally and Confidently

Take It Easy!

Second Edition

Herman Bartelen

Teacher's Manual

7. Do a dictation activity based on any one or two of the conversations. Students must write out the conversations while they are listening to the teacher read them out loud. The audio recording can also be used.

8. Do a "running dictation" activity. Put students into pairs and tape a conversation onto a wall somewhere in the class. One student from each pair must dictate the whole conversation to a partner by reading the short script and then running to the partner to dictate what he or she remembers.

Teaching Each Unit

Below are general instructions for teaching the main sections of each unit.

Opening Page *8–15 minutes in total*

This page introduces students to the main language that will be featured in the unit.

Cartoon *3–5 minutes*

The cartoon is designed to introduce one of the language items being introduced in the unit. These should be dealt with briefly. Animals, birds, insects, and sea creatures are the focus for these cartoons.

▶ **Basic Teaching Plan**

Read the cartoon out loud, or have students read the cartoon out loud to each other. Then, ask them questions about the cartoon: i.e. "Where are they?" "Why are they saying this?" "What is the situation?" "Is it funny to you?"

At the very beginning, explain the first cartoon by saying that many cartoons will have animals that speak. This is considered a valid and humorous way to comment on human and animal life.

Conversation Examples and Substitution Activity *5–10 minutes*

These conversation examples use language taken from the Building Blocks and Speaking Strategies sections. They provide students with conversations that they will learn and be able to use after the unit has been covered. It is not necessary to spend much time on these, but they should be covered as they allow students to speak confidently by completing the simple substitution exercises. As these examples occur every unit, it is important to ensure from the beginning that students know exactly what they need to do each time for this activity.

▶ **Basic Teaching Plan**

Establish the theme of the unit, and ask questions about it. Elicit the kind of language students might use. Read the conversations out loud and then have students complete the substitution exercises. Have student use the "Read, Look Up, Say" technique. When finished, answer any questions that they may have.

▶ **Alternative Teaching Approaches**

1. Model each of the conversations with a student. Then, have pairs of students do the substitution exercises.

2. Given that the two conversation examples are taken from each of the Building Blocks sections, it is possible to use the example conversation separately, and only when the class is focusing on that particular Building Block section.

3. Ask students to change the substitution words with those that reflect their own lives. Or, have them think creatively and change the words to whatever they wish.

4. Periodically, have students continue the conversations and guess as to what might follow the lines in the textbook.

These are the fundamental sections of the unit. They teach the language, expressions, and vocabulary necessary for dealing with the unit's themes and focus. This page has three different parts: key language, Listen In, and Speak Out.

(**Key Language**)   *10–15 minutes*

This part introduces the structures, phrases, vocabulary, and grammar necessary for dealing with the theme. These are also included in the Classroom Audio CD. This part is best taught and led by the teacher. The teacher should introduce the theme and then begin the process of having students read along with the CD, and repeat out loud the sentences and phrases. The role of the teacher is to ensure that this section is properly introduced. The teacher should ask students questions to ensure comprehension and answer any questions they may have. The CD provides a good pronunciation and rhythm model for the students.

▶ **Basic Teaching Plan**

Introduce the section's theme and explain the main points or grammar items. Next, have students listen to a recording of the phrases. Following this, students can read the sentences in this section out loud to each other. After this, have them close their books and then ask questions about the content. Use any of the following approaches:

1. Read the beginning of a sentence and then ask a student to complete the sentence. Or, for the sections that have questions and answers, read either the question or answer, and have a student give the other part.

2. Ask students to repeat any of the phrases or sentences that they remember. Correct if necessary.

▶ **Alternative Teaching Approaches**

1. Use the board to explain the main focus of the Building Block section. Choose examples from the textbook or use your own. Have students close their textbooks for this.

2. Play the CD for the students at first and then ask questions about the content. The students' textbooks can be open or closed.

(**Listen In**)   *10–15 minutes*

This part is designed to be short and uncomplicated, and is best led by the teacher. It is based entirely on the key language part from the Building Blocks section.

▶ **Basic Teaching Plan**

Pre-class preparation: Read the scripts and underline any vocabulary or expressions that the students might have trouble with. These can be pre-taught on the board.

First, read the instructions and make sure students understand. Then, play the CD two or three times and take up the answers. Write the answers on the board to ensure that all students have the correct answers. In addition, when taking up answers, read out loud the lines from the conversations that gives students the answer. After the answers are taken up, have students close their books, and play the CD one more time.

▶ **Alternative Teaching Approaches**

1. Introduce the activity and play the CD once. Take up one or two answers after the first listening. Then, play the CD again and take up the rest of the answers. When this is completed, have students close their textbooks and play the CD one more time.

2. Introduce the activity and play the CD once with textbooks closed. After this, elicit student answers to one or

two questions for each listening, but do not ask questions that are the same as in the textbook. The teacher can ask both questions for gist or main idea, or more detailed questions. Finally, play the CD again and have students complete the exercises in the textbook.

3. Photocopy the audio scripts for this part in this Teacher's Manual, and distribute them among students. Have pairs of students read the conversations out loud to each other. Then, have them complete the exercises in the textbook.

4. Photocopy the audio scripts for this part and make a cloze exercise. Have students listen and fill in the blanks. Take up the answers to the activity and then have students in pairs use the conversations to complete the exercises in the textbook. Finally, take up the answers.

(Speak Out) 10–15 minutes

This is a communicative student-centered activity and gives students the chance to use the language they have learned.

▶ Basic Teaching Plan

Read the instructions out loud with the class, and make sure these are clear to all students. Model one part of the activity with one student in order to provide an example. Then, have students do the activity. As students are doing the activity, walk around the class and make sure that the students are on task.

The teacher should also interact with students. At the end of the activity, get feedback from students and/or ask questions in order to personalize the activity. Answer any questions that they may have.

A good way to deal with error correction is for the teacher to walk around the class as students are doing the activity and write down some of the common mistakes that occur. Write some of these on the board and explain them to the students. If there is not enough time, take up the mistakes orally.

Be sure that students talk with many partners. By the end of the course of study, students should have talked several times with each of the students in class.

▶ Alternative Teaching Approaches

1. After the activity is over, have students write one or two short conversations based on the theme. Make sure that each student has a legible copy of the conversations in order to read these with other students. Move students around quickly as they read their conversations with each other. An alternative to this is to have students create conversations and send digital copies to the teacher. The teacher can then quickly edit and compile the conversations in a simple document that can be used for reading practice in the next class.

2. If the activity is based on questions on the unit's theme, have students write two or three of their own questions. Then, switch questions with another group and use them to talk with a partner. One alternative is to create a 9-square grid that can have a question or topic in each box. When these are exchanged with other groups, students can have a conversation or discussion based on the new questions.

3. Create or have the students write alternative questions or topics. Put these on slips of paper that are cut into strips. Then, re-distribute these to each pair or small group. Students take turns turning over the question papers, reading them out loud and answering the questions.

4. Vary the way students respond through one of the methods below.

   a. Students stand up and read conversations with different partners. Have them change partners several times.

   b. Students read conversations as if they were in one of the following moods: sad, happy, indifferent, angry, or confident. This is to internalize and practice emotional aspects of the language.

   c. Students read the conversations in both low and loud voices.

This section is designed to give students strategies and skills that help them manage conversation more confidently, and is similar to the Building Blocks sections.

(**Key Language**) *10 minutes*

The first part gives students the language focus for the page. This part is probably best led and introduced by the teacher. This is followed by two Speak Out activities.

▶ **Basic Teaching Plan**

Introduce the theme. Then, have students look at the vocabulary box while you play the CD. Next, have students read the sentences out loud to each other. Take up any questions and ask students questions to ensure comprehension.

▶ **Alternative Teaching Approaches**

Introduce the theme. Then, have students read the sentences in this part out loud to each other. After this, have them close their books and then ask questions about the content. Use any of the following approaches:

1. Read the beginning of a sentence and then asks a student to complete the sentence. Or, for the parts that have questions and answers, read either the question or answer, and have a student give the other part.

2. Ask students to repeat any of the phrases or sentences that they remember. Correct if necessary.

(**Speak Out**) *10–15 minutes*

This part consists of two activities that allow students to practice the strategy being taught.

▶ **Basic Teaching Plan**

Go over the instructions for each one separately and clarify what students are to do. Have students do the activities with a partner and move them around as much as possible in order to talk to different classmates.

▶ **Alternative Teaching Approaches**

When finished all the Speak Out activities, ask pairs of students to write one or two short conversations based on the theme. Make sure that each student has a legible copy of the conversations in order to read these with other students. Move students around as they read their conversations with each other.

Wrap It Up *10–20 minutes in total*

There is only one activity for this page, and it varies for each unit depending on the theme. The activity should allow students to use the language they have learned, and the teacher should briefly review the unit's contents, including the speaking strategy, before doing the final activity.

▶ **Basic Teaching Plan**

Read the instructions and be certain that students know what is required. Put students in pairs or in small groups, and have them complete the activity. The teacher's role will be to monitor, do periodic corrections of student mistakes, and write down some of the problems that students are encountering. The students' mistakes should be discussed at the end. When the activity is over, and as a whole-class activity, ask a few of the same questions of the students, or have students answer a question by raising their hands.

▶ Alternative Teaching Approaches

1. At the beginning of the activity, have students ask the teacher any of the questions. By doing so, the teacher can give model answers using vocabulary from the unit.

2. For the activities that have a list of questions, have students write their own additional questions. Make sure that these can then be used with other students.

3. Have students write short conversations based on their talks. The teacher can correct these as the students are writing them. Be sure to share these with other students.

Word Bank

This section contains the important vocabulary from the unit. Vocabulary development is an important feature in any language-learning program, and the Word Bank should be reviewed by students, and used by the teacher whenever possible. The parts of speech were emphasized in order to show that students need to be fully aware of the functions of words. It is best used before a unit is taught. The second edition of *Take It Easy!* has Japanese translations for this section. The lists can be copied and shared with students. By having a Japanese translation, students will be clear as to the meanings of the words.

▶ Basic Teaching Plan

Before class, the teacher should quickly check the words, as some words or phrases are used in a particular way in the unit. The teacher can ask students to look at the lists and check any words that they don't know either in class or at home. Ask students to check the words they know. They should then look up the words in a dictionary and write down the definitions, preferably in English. If the Word Bank is covered in class, the teacher can explain the words to the students. Some of the vocabulary is used again in other units.

▶ Alternative Teaching Approaches

1. As homework, have students review the vocabulary before they come to class. Take up any questions at the beginning of class.

2. Say the words out loud and have students repeat. Answer any questions they may have.

3. Vocabulary Notebook: Have students keep a vocabulary notebook for unknown words from the textbook.

4. In pairs, have students look at a vocabulary list for a unit. Then, have students ask questions and give answers with the aim to use all of the vocabulary on the page. This activity can be treated as a competition as the first students to use every word from the page are declared the winners.

Using the Reviews

The review sections occur every three units and are designed to review the language and vocabulary taught up to that point. The teacher has the choice of using these for assessment purposes or simply as a review of what has been taught. There are four or five Speak Out activities and two Listen In activities.

▶ Basic Teaching Plan

Remind students of what they have learned in the previous three units. Ask questions of students or use the board to write down key points. Tell students that they will do several challenging activities that test their knowledge and memory of what they have learned.

Speak Out 1

This activity will always have three conversations with blanks for missing words. There is a word list that students can use to fill in the blanks.

▶ Basic Teaching Plan

Explain the activity to the students and have them complete each of the conversations. When finished, the teacher can take up the answers. Finally, have students read the conversations to each other.

Speak Out 2

This activity will always have boxes with topic words written inside.

▶ Basic Teaching Plan

Students must talk in English about a topic for at least 1 minute without stopping. They should concentrate on saying whatever comes to mind but stick close to the topic theme.

▶ Alternative Teaching Approaches

1. After a student has finished talking for one minute, another student can ask one or two questions.
2. For each review, increase the time that students have to talk. By the end of the book, they should be able to speak for two minutes or more on any of the topics.

Speak Out 3, 4, 5

These activities vary but deal with the themes and vocabulary from the previous three units. Two activities are essential for students.

Presentations (Speak Out 3 or 4)

Students will be asked to give prepared presentations on the certain topics. These are best done in small groups of three or four students.

▶ Basic Teaching Plan

It is essential that the teacher gives a clear introduction and explanation of how to do presentations in class. There should be clear rules for the following:

1. Students should look at the guidelines given for each presentation.
2. The teacher needs to decide if students need to memorize or are able to use notes. Using notes is fine if the "Read, Look Up, Say" technique is used.
3. The length for each presentation should be clearly established. The teacher needs to decide what to do if students go longer than the scheduled time. Giving an extra 30 seconds after the timer has run is acceptable.
4. Assign other students in the group to ask questions when a presentation is done.
5. Presentations can be used for assessment also.
6. Have students do their presentations two or three times and for different groups of students each time.

15 Free-speaking Questions (Speak Out 4 or 5)

The final Speak Out activity for each review is a list of 15 questions.

▶Basic Teaching Plan

Explain what students will need to do for this activity. Students must answer each of the questions with at least two sentences and there should be follow-up questions from the other students. It is advisable to make sure that each student in the group both asks and answers questions.

▶Alternative Teaching Approaches

1. Put students into groups of three. Assign five questions to each of the students. The student who is asking questions is the only one who can look at the questions. The other students must listen and answer. The student who asks the questions must also ask follow-up questions.

2. Put each question on its own strip of paper or on a small rectangular card. Place these cards face down on one of the students' desks. The first card is turned over. Student A asks the question, Student B answers the question, and Student C asks follow-up questions. The order then changes for the next question.

Downloadable Teacher's Resources

The following resources are available at the National Geographic Learning | Cengage Learning website:

Audio Scripts

All the audio scripts for the Listen In activities are compiled into a single document.

Word Bank with Japanese Translations

The Word Bank pages of all 12 units from this Teacher's Manual are compiled into a single document.

You can download these resources at:

http://www.cengagejapan.com/elt/ListeningSpeaking/

1. Go to the website above.
2. Click the cover image or the book title (Take It Easy! Second Edition).
3. Click "Instructor Site (教師用サイト)" and then put in the ID and Password issued by National Geographic Learning | Cengage Learning.
4. Click the link to download.

Special Activities

Below are supplementary activities for any unit in the textbook. There are five sections: Speaking, Listening, Using the Audio Scripts, Using the Word Bank, and Games.

Speaking

Activity 1 | Questions on Cards

It is possible to use questions from the unit in a different way. The 15 questions from the review sections are especially good for this. First, take a set of questions from the textbook, re-type them, print and cut each question separately. Then, glue the strip of paper with the question onto a small rectangular card. For this activity, do the following:

1. Put students in groups of 3.
2. One student turns over a card and reads the question.
3. The second student answers the question with at least two sentences.
4. The third student asks a question related to the second student's answer.

Activity 2 | Read, Look Up, Say

An important thing to remember is to encourage students to use the "Read, Look Up, Say" technique, in which students look at a line or two of a conversation, look up at their partner and then say the line from memory. This technique works to enforce the memorization of conversations, and discourages students from only reading lines in a monotone voice.

Activity 3 | Timed Answers

Anytime that students do a speaking activity that has questions, have the student who is not answering time the response and ensure that the person talking speaks for a certain amount of time. A suggested time is 30 seconds.

Activity 4 | Short Impromptu Presentations

Choose any theme or topic from the unit, and give students a short amount of time (preferably 5–10 minutes) to prepare a 2-minute presentation. Put the students into small groups and have them give their short presentations. Change groups two or three times.

Activity 5 | Writing Conversations

Put students into pairs and have them write a conversation between two people about the unit's topic. The students must then memorize and say their conversations out loud in front of the class. An alternate activity is to have students use a minimum number of expressions from the textbook's unit.

Activity 6 | Questionnaires

Questionnaires are good, communicative activities. The simplest way to deal with questionnaires is as follows:

1. Put students in pairs and have them create a survey of 5–10 questions based on a topic from the unit's theme. After being checked by the teacher, students can then use their questionnaires with the other students in class. Students can take notes for the responses and later share the results.

2. When finished, students can then summarize the results and share these with the whole class.

Activity 7 **Oral Repetition without Looking at the Textbook**

For this activity, students must close their textbooks. Use any passage or example from the textbook and have students repeat after you read out each sentence. This activity forces students to concentrate and pay attention to what they hear. Students don't have to repeat too loudly as it might cause confusion in the classroom, especially if students make mistakes.

Activity 8 **Across-Class Conversations**

This activity is based on any of the conversations in the textbook or audio scripts. Students are divided into As and Bs. Each pair stands across from each other on opposite sides of the room. Have students practice a conversation and say the sentences loudly. This activity is noisy, but it will help students develop confidence to speak English in a loud voice. This activity could also be used for cloze activities.

Activity 9 **Stand and Read**

Students stand and start reading an example conversation at the same time. When a student finishes reading, they sit down. This can also be a competition to see who can read the fastest.

Activity 10 **Rewriting Questions**

In pairs, have students choose 5–10 questions from a section from the textbook, and then make small changes to each of the questions. Then, with another partner, use the questions for discussion. This is good practice for writing questions.

Activity 11 **Topic Grid**

Create a grid of 4 x 4 on an A4 piece of paper. Distribute the sheet to groups of two or three students. Have them write down topics for discussion in each of the empty rectangles on the grid. They should be based on themes studied in class. Then, re-distribute the grids so that each group now has a different set of topics. Students must then talk about or discuss the topics. One good alternative is to have students talk about each topic for a set amount of time.

Listening

Activity 12 **Cloze Listening**

For this activity, the teacher needs an enlarged copy of the audio scripts from one section of the textbook. The teacher then erases certain words and draw lines for students to write in the words they hear. In the classroom, the teacher can then either read or play a recording of the conversations. While listening, students fill in the blanks. The teacher can repeat the conversations several times. When finished, correct the answers, and then have students read the conversations to each other.

Activity 13 **Dictation**

Similar to the cloze listening exercise, the teacher can also do dictation activities for any of the conversations or groups of conversations. This will definitely help students improve listening skills. The common procedure for doing dictation is as follows:

1. Choose 1–3 conversations from the audio scripts.

2. Do three readings of each conversation.

3. For the first reading, say the conversation naturally.

4. For the second reading, speak more slowly and allow students time to write down what they hear.

5. For the final reading, read the conversation naturally again. If necessary, you can read for a fourth time.

6. Finally, take up the answers.

Activity 14 | Running Dictation

This is also a dictation activity, but students will be the ones doing the dictating. It is called Running Dictation because students will be trying to win the game by running quickly. It is a lively and fun, competitive activity. The procedure is as follows:

1. Make enough copies of a conversation for each pair of students in the class.

2. Put or tape the conversations somewhere in the classroom.

3. One student must read the conversation and then choose several words or sentences to dictate to their partner who is sitting in a different part of the classroom. Students should run fast in order to win the competition.

4. The student then dictates to their partner what they remember, and the other partner must write down what they hear on a piece of paper. The "running'" student cannot help or correct.

5. This continues until the whole conversation has been dictated after which time, the students can check their answers. Give points for being first or second to finish, but take away points for each mistake.

Using the Audio Scripts

Activity 15 | Reading Audio Scripts Out Loud

At the beginning of the term of study, make one copy of the audio scripts for all units for each student. After finishing the listening activity for any unit, have students take out the scripts and read them to each other. Be sure to use the "Read, Look Up, Say" technique. To save paper, send a PDF copy to the students; they can use their phones for reading in class.

Activity 16 | Shadowing

Shadowing, or repeating, what is said by the teacher or the audio recording is good for developing both listening and speaking skills. Students must have both the audio scripts and access to the audio recording. Students listen to and read a sentence from a conversation, stop the recording and then repeat the sentence. When repeating, students should aim to copy the pronunciation, intonation, and stress patterns of the speaker. Shadowing is a very easy and useful technique for students to learn and practice in their free time. The first time you introduce this to the students, have them practice in class.

Using the Word Bank

Activity 17 | Testing Vocabulary

At the beginning of the term of study, make one copy of the Word Bank that has both the English and Japanese translations. For this simple activity, put students into pairs. One student will have the list of words in both Japanese and English. This student says the Japanese translation for a word and the other student has to say the

English translation. This activity is good for reinforcing and reviewing vocabulary for each unit. To save paper, send a PDF copy to the students so that they can use their phones or computers in class.

▶ **Alternative: Matching Words Test**

The teacher can create tests for checking vocabulary by using the document for a unit's Word Bank. The teacher can create a matching test by putting the English words on the left side and the Japanese translations on the right side. Students must match the English words with their correct Japanese translations.

| Activity 18 | **Spelling Bee**

Take the words in the Word Bank and have a Spelling Bee contest. If the class is large, have students divide into small groups with one person who is the MC and activity leader. An introduction to this activity should explain the common use of Spelling Bees in English-speaking culture. There are now national student Spelling Bees in many countries.

Games

| Activity 19 | **Jumbled Conversations**

This activity is fun and challenging, and is based on conversations from the textbook or audio scripts. The procedure is as follows:

1. Re-type the lines from a conversation.

2. Cut the conversation into strips. Each strip will have one line from the conversation.

3. Put a paper clip on all the lines from one conversation. You will need to make as many copies as you need for your class.

4. Distribute the conversation strips to each group and have them put the lines in the correct order. It is best to have three or four conversations ready when you do this activity.

▶ **Alternative: Really Jumbled Conversations**

If you wish to challenge your students, do the following:

1. Put three or four conversations together and have them put all conversations together correctly. The teacher can walk around the class and help students when necessary.

2. Type the jumbled conversations into a Word document and show each one on a screen in class. Number each sentence so that students can put the sentences in the correct order easily.

| Activity 20 | **A Crossword Puzzle**

The teacher can create a crossword puzzle using the words in Word Bank. There are many online sites that allow teachers to create crossword puzzles for class use. This would be very good for review at the end of three units of study. To simplify the workload, get definitions from a simple ESL dictionary that you have or access online.

| Activity 21 | **Password**

This activity is based on an older famous TV game show from America. For this activity, the class can use one unit from the Word Bank. The activity is played as follows:

1. One student (Student A) looks at a section of words from the Word Bank. The other student (Student B) cannot look at the word list.

2. Student A then chooses one word from the section and tries to give verbal clues so that Student B can guess what the word is. Student A can use phrases like: "It's a person." "You can see it in a supermarket." "It's red." "It's a verb." "You do this when you wake up in the morning."

3. This continues until the teacher says "Stop." A recommended length of time is two or three minutes depending on the number of words used. Then, students count up the number of words that they guessed right.

4. Students switch roles and use a different section of the Word Bank.

5. This continues for several rounds. After finishing, students can add up their total score in order to determine the winners.

▶ Alternative 1: Gesture Password

A fun alternative is to have students use gestures only in Step 2. Student B has to guess the word based on the gestures Student A makes. This can be very funny and interesting.

▶ Alternative 2: Drawing Password

Another enjoyable alternative is to have students use drawings only in Step 2. Student B has to guess the word based on a drawing.

Answers

Audio Scripts

Word Bank with Japanese Translations

Themes: Meeting and greeting people
Grammar items: Present tense questions and answers
Speaking skills: Hesitating

Building Blocks 1   Student Book: p. 8

Listen In

Answers

Know each other: 1, 4   Are meeting for the first time: 2, 3

Audio Scripts

1. ► Audio: A-03

A: Alice, how are you?
B: Not bad. And you?
A: Fantastic.

2. ► Audio: A-04

A: Hi. Nice to meet you.
B: Nice to meet you, too.
A: Are you enjoying the party?
B: Yeah. It's fun.

3. ► Audio: A-05

A: Hi.
B: Hi. How are you doing?
A: Pretty good.
B: Are you from around here?
A: Yes. I go to school here. My name is Jim, by the way.
B: Hi, Jim. My name is Aya.
A: Hi, Aya. So, what do you study?

4. ► Audio: A-06

A: Good morning.
B: Good morning, Jane. How's it going?
A: All right, but I'm in a hurry.
B: Okay. I'll see you on Friday.
A: Yeah. Take it easy.
B: See you.

Speak Out

Answers

❶ afternoon, introduce, Nice, pleased
❷ How, you, So, Sounds, Bye

Listen In

Answers

1. No
2. are
3. like
4. does
5. to
6. it's on

Audio Scripts

▶ Audio: A-09

1. Is the teacher American?
2. Are they from New Zealand?
3. What do you like to do in your free time?
4. Does she have a part-time job?
5. Where do we have to study?
6. Is the test on Monday?

Speak Out

Answers

1. What
2. Does
3. Why
4. When
5. Where
6. Do
7. Is
8. Who
9. Are

Japanese Translations

Useful Phrases

Take it easy.　じゃあね。
See you later.　また、あとで。
Sounds good.　いいね。
Pretty good.　すごくいいね。
Yeah.　うん。
How about you?　あなたはどうなの？
And you?　あなたは？
Anyway, …　とにかく、…
Well, …　ええと、…
So, …　それで、…
by the way　ちなみに
in my free time　空き時間に
around here　この辺

Nouns

Monday　月曜日
Tuesday　火曜日
Wednesday　水曜日
Thursday　木曜日
Friday　金曜日
Saturday　土曜日
Sunday　日曜日
today　今日
morning　朝、午前
afternoon　午後
evening　夜
breakfast　朝食
lunch　昼食
dinner　夕食
supper　夕食
family　家族
parents　両親
father　父親
mother　母親
brother　兄、弟
sister　姉、妹
grandfather　祖父
grandmother　祖母
grandchild　孫

relative　親類
uncle　おじ
aunt　おば
cousin　いとこ
nephew　おい
niece　めい
everyone　みんな
best friend　親友
classmate　級友
student　生徒
home　家
apartment　アパート、マンション
train station　駅
area　地域
building　建物
library　図書館
school　学校
period　(授業などの) 時間
subject　教科
major　専攻
Korean　韓国語

Verbs

be born　生まれる
be in a hurry　急いでいる
live　住む
live by *oneself*　一人暮らしをする
have　持っている、…がある
have a test　試験がある
have a part-time job
　　　　　　　アルバイトをしている
do　する
want to do *something*　…をしたい
ride *one's* bike　自転車に乗る
buy　買う
go out　出かける
cook　料理する
study　勉強する
work　働く
complete　完成する
meet　会う

greet　あいさつする
introduce　紹介する
hesitate　ためらう
spend time with *someone*
　　　　　　　…と一緒に過ごす
love　大好きである
like　好きである
dislike　嫌いである

Adjectives

American　アメリカの
Australian　オーストラリアの
British　イギリスの
Canadian　カナダの
English　英語の
European　ヨーロッパの
Irish　アイルランドの
New Zealand　ニュージーランドの
Scottish　スコットランドの
Welsh　ウェールズの
useful　役に立つ
nice　良い

Adverbs and Prepositions

near　近くに
close to　近接して、親密で
usually　たいてい、ふだんは

Unit 2 Growing Up

Themes: Talking about the past
Grammar items: Past tense questions and answers
Speaking skills: Showing interest

Building Blocks 1 Student Book: p. 14

Listen In

Answers

1. grew, outside, friends
2. liked, elementary, sports
3. born, lived, 14

Audio Scripts

1. ▶ Audio: A-11

   A: So, where did you grow up, Tom?
   B: I grew up in the countryside. There were a lot of rice fields and mountains.
   A: Sounds beautiful. Did you like it?
   B: Oh, yeah. It was fun. My friends and I always played outside near the river. It was beautiful.

2. ▶ Audio: A-12

   A: Did you like elementary school, Lisa?
   B: Yes, very much.
   A: So, what subjects did you like?
   B: Well, I liked all subjects actually, but I wasn't very good at sports.
   A: Me, neither.

3. ▶ Audio: A-13

   A: Where were you born, Alex?
   B: I was born in Osaka, but I grew up in New York City. My father worked there.
   A: That's interesting. How long did you live there?
   B: For 14 years.
   A: Wow!

Speak Out

Answers

1. was
2. Did
3. Were
4. was
5. did
6. did
7. were
8. did
9. Did
10. Did

Listen In

Answers

1. used to, Sunday, make lunches
2. loved, watch, take
3. sister, play loud, high school, danced
4. climbed, go hiking, never climbed

Audio Scripts

1. ▸ Audio: A-16

A: You know, when I was young, I used to play baseball with my friends every Sunday.
B: You're kidding! Every Sunday?
A: Yeah. I remember that our mothers used to make lunches for us. It was so much fun.

2. ▸ Audio: A-17

A: When I was young, I loved basketball and I always used to watch it on TV.
B: That's interesting. Did you play on a team?
A: No, but I wanted to. My father used to take me to basketball games, though.

3. ▸ Audio: A-18

A: I used to listen to music all the time when I was a high school student.
B: Really?
A: Yeah. We were living in a house, and my sister and I always played loud music. Our friends often came over and we used to dance.
B: Wow! Did your parents get angry with you?
A: Not really. They thought it was cute.

4. ▸ Audio: A-19

A: Have you ever climbed Mt. Fuji?
B: Yeah, once. I did it when I was in high school.
A: Wow!
B: It was very difficult. How about you? Have you ever climbed Mt. Fuji?
A: Never. My family used to go hiking, but we never climbed Mt. Fuji.

Japanese Translations

Useful Phrases

when I was younger 私が若いころ
when I was six years old
　　　　　　　　　　　　私が６歳のとき
at the time 当時
so far これまで、今のところ
for 14 years 14年間
all the time いつでも
every summer 毎夏
every weekend 毎週末
after school 放課後
at home 家で

Nouns

kindergarten 幼稚園
elementary school 小学校
junior high school 中学校
high school 高校
memory 思い出
summer holiday 夏休み
school trip 修学旅行
subject 教科
interest 興味
volleyball バレーボール
baseball 野球
basketball バスケットボール
sketchbook スケッチブック
comic book 漫画本
city 都会
countryside 田舎
rice field 田んぼ
chopsticks 箸
sweets 菓子
finger 指
thumb 親指

Verbs

be born 生まれる
grow up 成長する

graduate from …を卒業する
get married 結婚する
live with *someone* …と一緒に住む
be good at *something* …が得意である
be bad at *something* …が苦手である
remember 覚えている
enjoy 楽しむ
collect *something* …を集める
listen to music 音楽を聴く
play music （音楽を）演奏する
play in a band バンドで演奏する
play *one's* CD CDをかける
dye *one's* hair 髪を染める
fall asleep 眠りに落ちる
go to bed 就寝する
put on clothes 服を着る
make lunch 昼食を作る
cook 料理する
read 読む
draw 描く
dance 踊る
carry 持ち運ぶ
travel 旅行する
travel abroad 海外旅行をする
go camping キャンプに行く
go hiking ハイキングに行く
go out 出かける
come over やって来る
give *someone something*
　　　　　　　　　…に〜をあげる
take *someone* to *a place or activity*
　　　　　　　…を〜に連れて行く
hang out with *someone*
　　　　　　　　　…と一緒に遊ぶ
play hide and seek かくれんぼをする
climb a tree 木に登る
ride a bicycle 自転車に乗る
have an accident 事故に遭う
fall down 落ちる
break an arm 腕を折る
break a bone 骨折する
cry 泣く

hurt 痛む
quit やめる

Adjectives

beautiful 美しい
cute かわいい
fun 楽しい
boring つまらない
easy 簡単な
difficult 難しい
important 大切な
unimportant 重要でない
favorite 大好きな
loud 大音量の、騒がしい
quiet 静かな

Adverbs and Prepositions

especially 特に
inside 屋内で
outside 外で
early 早く
late 遅く

Themes: Daily routines / Personal news
Grammar items: Adverbs of frequency / "How" questions
Speaking skills: Talking about personal news / Asking questions

Building Blocks 1   Student Book: p. 20

Listen In

Answers

1. always, often, usually, sometimes
2. always, almost always, often, never
3. often, usually, sometimes, hardly ever
4. usually, sometimes, not … very often, rarely

Audio Scripts

1. ▶ Audio: A-21

A: Where do you usually go after school?
B: I go to the gym to work out.
A: That's great! How often do you go?
B: I always go on Tuesdays and Thursdays, and I sometimes work out on Fridays, too.

2. ▶ Audio: A-22

A: Well, school is over for today. What are you going to do?
B: I think I'll go to the library and study.
A: Really? Do you often study in the library?
B: Yeah. Akiko and I almost always study there after school.
A: I never go to the library to study. I always study at home.

3. ▶ Audio: A-23

A: What do you usually do after school?
B: It depends. I often hang out with my friends at school, and I sometimes work at my part-time job. How about you?
A: Well, I hardly ever stay at school. I usually go home and have dinner. After that, I chat with my friends online or watch videos on the Internet.

4. ▶ Audio: A-24

A: When do you do the laundry?
B: Um … I sometimes do it on the weekends, but I usually do it during the week. And you?
A: Well, I rarely do it during the week because I'm too busy. Actually, I don't do the laundry very often.
B: How come?
A: My mom does it for me.

Speak Out 1

Sample Answers

❶ What are, Wow, when
❷ Guess, I didn't know that, so that
❸ That's too bad, what, because

Building Blocks 2   Student Book: p. 22

Listen In

Answers

1. Twice a year.
2. About five minutes.
3. Thirty dollars.
4. About four or five hours of homework.

Audio Scripts

1. ► Audio: A-27

   A: I don't want to but I'm going to clean my room tonight.
   B: Really? How often do you clean your room?
   A: Not very often. I clean my room … ah … twice a year.
   B: You're kidding!

2. ► Audio: A-28

   A: I usually ride my motorbike to the station.
   B: Really? And how long does it take you to get to the station?
   A: About five minutes.

3. ► Audio: A-29

   A: My father's going to take us to a soccer game tonight.
   B: That's fantastic! How much does it cost for a ticket to a soccer game?
   A: It usually costs 30 dollars.
   B: Wow! That's cheap!

4. ► Audio: A-30

   A: Guess what! Our teacher gave us more homework to do.
   B: That's too bad. Your teacher gives you a lot of homework, doesn't he?
   A: Well, it depends, but we usually have to do about four or five hours of homework every week.
   B: Really? That's a lot!

Japanese Translations

Useful Phrases

Guess what! ちょっと聞いて！
It depends. 場合による。
Really? ほんとうに？
Wow! すごい！
That's fantastic! 最高だね！
That's great! いいね！
You're kidding. 冗談を言って。
That's too bad! 気の毒に。
That's terrible. ひどい。
Oh no! なんてこと！
How much does it cost?
　　　　　　　いくらかかる？

Actually, … 実際のところ、…
Anyway, … いずれにしても、…
at home 家で
at school 学校で
six hours a day 1日に６時間
once a week 週に1回
twice a month 月に２回
three times a year 年に３回
in the mornings 午前中には
in the evenings 夜には
on Mondays 月曜日には
every Friday 毎週金曜日に
every day 毎日
on purpose わざと
nowadays 今日では
these days このごろ

Nouns

hometown 故郷の町
mom お母さん
dad お父さん
room key 部屋の鍵
motorbike オートバイ
gym （スポーツ）ジム
game ゲーム、試合
ticket チケット
crime show 刑事ドラマ

comedy show お笑い番組
variety show バラエティ番組
news ニュース
news reporter ニュース記者
frequency 頻度
social media ソーシャルメディア

Verbs

be over 終わる
finish 終わらせる
express 表現する
respond 応答する
forget 忘れる
miss 受け損なう
lose 紛失する
steal 盗む
take [人に時間を] 要する
ride a bike 自転車に乗る
walk to the station 駅まで歩く
get to school 学校に着く
go home 家に帰る
do housework 宿題をする
do the laundry 洗濯をする
do the dishes 食器を洗う
iron アイロンをかける
clean one's room 部屋を掃除する
put out the garbage ごみを出す
cook for someone …のために料理をする
eat breakfast 朝食をとる
take a shower シャワーを浴びる
wash one's hair 髪を洗う
sleep in late 遅くまで寝る
play music （音楽を）演奏する
play a video game テレビゲームをする
go for a walk 散歩に行く
hang out with someone …と遊ぶ
date 付き合う、交際する
work out 体を鍛える、運動する
buy 買う
spend money 金を使う
cost 2,000 yen 2000円かかる

cost 30 dollars 30ドルかかる
cost for something …に [いくら] かかる
work at a part-time job
　　　　　　　アルバイトをする
study abroad 海外に留学する
get 700 on the TOEIC test
　　TOEICテストで700点を取る

Adjectives

American アメリカの
British イギリスの
Japanese 日本の
small 小さい
big 大きい
cheap 安い、安価な
expensive 高い、高価な
busy 忙しい

Adverbs and Prepositions

always いつも
almost always ほぼいつも
often しばしば、頻繁に
usually たいてい、ふだんは
sometimes ときどき
not … very often それほど頻繁に…しない
rarely めったに…しない
hardly ever まずめったに…しない
never けっして…しない

Review for Units 1–3

Speak Out 1 Student Book: pp. 25–26

Answers

❶ Hello, How, Pretty, Are, Yes, by, name, So
❷ grow, grew, Sounds, fun, How, up, was, Did, used, go, Really, still
❸ What, usually, sometimes, often, have, twice, about, Do, every, kidding

Speak Out 3 Student Book: pp. 26–27

Answers

1. do 2. do 3. are 4. Do 5. Do 6. did 7. did 8. were 9. Was 10. did 11. do 12. do

Listen In 1 Student Book: p. 28

Answers

1. **a)** At a party. **b)** No.
2. **a)** Terrible. **b)** He got sick last night.
3. **a)** In London. **b)** For 12 years.
4. **a)** Twice. **b)** He got really sick.
5. **a)** She will eat and study. **b)** The woman.
6. **a)** Go to a baseball game on the weekend. **b)** Forty dollars.

Audio Scripts

1. ▶ Audio: A-31

  A: Hi. Nice to meet you.
  B: Nice to meet you, too.
  A: Are you enjoying the party?
  B: It's great. Do you want to dance?
  A: Sure.

2. ▶ Audio: A-32

  A: Amy, how are you?
  B: Not bad. And you?
  A: Terrible.
  B: Why? What happened?
  A: I got sick last night and couldn't study for the test.
  B: That's too bad. I hope you feel better.

3. ▶ Audio: A-33

  A: Where were you born, Emma?
  B: I was born in London, but I grew up in Osaka. My father worked there.
  A: That's interesting. How long did you live there?
  B: For 12 years.
  A: Wow!

4. ▶ Audio: A-34

  A: Have you ever been to Hong Kong?
  B: Yeah, twice. I traveled there with my family once, and once on a school trip.
  A: Wow! Did you like it?
  B: It's an interesting place. I went to Disneyland with my family. That was great. But I got really sick on our school trip.
  A: That's too bad.

5. ▶ Audio: A-35

  A: Well, school is over for today. What are you going to do?
  B: I think I'll go home, eat and then study.
  A: Really? Do you like studying at home?
  B: Yeah. I like my room. I never go to the library to study. Do you use the library?
  A: All the time.

6. ▶ Audio: A-36

  A: My father's going to take the family to a baseball game on the weekend.
  B: That's fantastic! How much does it cost for a ticket to a baseball game?
  A: It usually costs 40 dollars.
  B: Wow! That's cheap!

Answers

1. **a)** T   **b)** F (They will meet on Saturday.)
2. **a)** F (The man grew up in Saitama Prefecture.)
   b) F (The man lived in Tokyo for two years. / The man lived near Gumma Prefecture for about 14 years.)
3. **a)** F (The woman belonged to the volleyball club in high school.)
   b) F (She belonged to the volleyball club for six years.)
4. **a)** F (One of the speakers played soccer when they were young.)
   b) F (One of the speakers has seen a professional soccer game.)
5. **a)** T   **b)** T
6. **a)** T   **b)** F (The speaker and his friends do their homework together at a restaurant.)

Audio Scripts

1. ▶ Audio: A-37

   A: Good morning.
   B: Good morning, Jane. How's it going?
   A: All right, but I'm in a hurry.
   B: Okay. I'll see you on Friday.
   A: Sorry. I can't make it Friday. Is Saturday okay?
   B: Of course. Until then, see you.
   A: Yeah. Take it easy.

2. ▶ Audio: A-38

   I was born in Tokyo but I grew up in Saitama. We lived near Gumma Prefecture. We lived near the mountains so it was quite beautiful. It was really hot in summer, though. Up to 40 degrees sometimes. Let's see. I lived there for about 14 years, and we lived in Tokyo for two years.

3. ▶ Audio: A-39

   A: Did you like junior high school, Jane?
   B: Yes, very much.
   A: Did you belong to any clubs?
   B: I belonged to the brass band club and also the volleyball club. I was in the music club for only three months. It was too difficult. I was a member of the volleyball team every year in junior high school.
   A: Wow! Did you play volleyball in high school, too?
   B: Yup, all three years. I loved it.

4. ▶ Audio: A-40

   A: You know, when I was young, I used to play soccer with my friends every Sunday.
   B: You're kidding! Every Sunday?
   A: Yeah. I remember that our mothers used to make lunches for us. It was so much fun.
   B: When I was young, I loved soccer too and I always used to watch it on TV.
   A: Did you play on a team?
   B: No, but I wanted to. My father used to take me to soccer games, though.
   A: Lucky you. I've never seen a professional soccer game.

5. ▶ Audio: A-41

   A: Guess what! Our history teacher gave us more homework to do.
   B: That's too bad. He gives you a lot of homework, doesn't he?
   A: Well, it depends, but we usually have to do about four or five hours of homework every week.
   B: Really? That's a lot! My history teacher is not so strict and only gives us about one hour of homework every week.
   A: I want to be in your class!

6. ▶ Audio: A-42

   After school, I often hang out with my friends. We usually stay at school and talk. Sometimes I have a part-time job but that is always on Friday or Saturday. My friends and I like to hang out at the station. There's a cool restaurant there that we visit and sometimes we do homework. We don't meet much on the weekends because we are very busy with club activities.

Themes: Future plans / Free time activities
Grammar items: The future tense / The past tense
Speaking skills: Asking follow-up questions

Building Blocks 1   Student Book: p. 30

Listen In

Answers

1. in the mall near their home, tomorrow night at 6:30
2. see the Lions baseball game, gate, on Sunday at 6:00
3. go see a movie, at the café by the station, on Saturday at 5:15

Audio Scripts

1. ▶ Audio: A-44

A: What are your plans for tomorrow night?
B: Well, this is unusual but I'm going to go bowling with my family.
A: Really? That sounds fun. Where are you going to go?
B: The mall near our home. My father works until 5, so we're going to meet at 6:30. We're going to have dinner first.
A: That sounds like a good night.

2. ▶ Audio: A-45

A: Hi, Cathy. I have tickets for the Lions game on Sunday. Do you want to go?
B: I'd love to. I love baseball. What time does the game start?
A: It starts at 7:00, so let's meet at the gate of the stadium.
B: Okay. What time?
A: Let me see … is 6 o'clock okay?
B: Six is fine. At the gate of the Lions stadium.
A: That's right. Okay, I'll see you on Sunday. Bye for now.
B: See you.

3. ▶ Audio: A-46

A: What do you want to do on the weekend?
B: Let's go see a movie on Saturday.
A: That's a good idea. Where do you want to meet?
B: Let's meet at the café by the station.
A: Okay. What time shall we meet?
B: Is 5:15 okay?
A: That's fine. So, I'll see you at the café by the station at 5:15 on Saturday.

Speak Out

Answers

❶ want, going, sounds, let's

❷ plans, to do, feel, meet

Building Blocks 2   Student Book: p. 32

Listen In

Answers

1. went to the zoo, went hiking with family
2. went to Tokyo Skytree, went to an Italian restaurant with Naomi, went to see a Kabuki play
3. went on a boat ride, went swimming at the lake with high school friends, went for a long drive around the lake

---

Audio Scripts

1. ▶ Audio: A-49

   A: You look tired. What's up?

   B: Well, I had a busy weekend. On Saturday, I went to the zoo with my boyfriend.

   A: Sounds good, but I don't see why you're so tired.

   B: Well, on Sunday, I went hiking with my family and tried horseback riding.

   A: Wow. How was that?

   B: It was terrible. I wasn't comfortable and I felt so tired afterwards.

   A: You're getting old!

   B: I know.

2. ▶ Audio: A-50

   A: Hey, Pete. How was Sunday? I heard you had a big date.

   B: It was great. Naomi and I went to Tokyo Skytree. It was really beautiful.

   A: And what did you do after that?

   B: We had lunch at an Italian restaurant, and then we went to see a Kabuki play.

   A: How was that?

   B: Fantastic! If you have the chance, you should see it.

3. ▶ Audio: A-51

   A: What did you do on the 18th?

   B: Um … on the 18th? Let me see … oh yeah … I went on a boat ride.

   A: Really? How was it?

   B: It was great.

   A: Who did you go with?

   B: I went with some of my high school friends. It was very interesting. And after that, we went swimming at the lake.

   A: Wow. How did you get to the lake?

   B: My friend's brother drove us. Afterwards, we went for a long drive around the lake.

   A: Cool.

Word Bank Student Book: p. 34

Japanese Translations

Useful Phrases

Bye for now. じゃあ、また。
Of course. もちろん。
Sure. もちろん。
That's fine. それで大丈夫。
Sounds fine. うん、大丈夫。
Cool. すごい。
If you have the chance, …
　　　　　　　機会があったら、…
during the week 平日に
on the weekend 週末に
on the 21st 21日に
on Friday 金曜日に
in the morning 午前中に
at noon 正午に、昼に
in the afternoon 午後に
in the evening 夜に、夕方に
at night 夜に、夜間に
at 6:00 6時に
at 6 o'clock 6時ちょうどに
last week 先週
last Monday evening
　　　　　　　先週の月曜日の夜
the day before yesterday 一昨日
last night 昨夜
this morning 今朝
tonight 今夜
tomorrow morning 明日の朝
tomorrow night 明日の夜
the day after tomorrow 明後日
next week 来週
It depends. 一概には言えない。

Nouns

invitation 招待
preference 好み
hot spring 温泉
amusement park 遊園地
stadium 競技場
gate 入り口

zoo 動物園
zebra シマウマ

Verbs

suppose 仮定する
try 挑戦する、試す
chase 追いかける
invite 招待する
meet 会う
be in good shape 体調が良い
be in bad shape 体調が悪い
look tired 疲れているように見える
take it easy のんびりする
sleep in ゆっくり寝る
stay overnight 夜更かしする
feel like doing *something*
　　　　　　　…したい気分である
prefer to do *something*
　　　　　　　…をするほうがいい
do *one's* schoolwork 宿題をする
clean *one's* room 部屋を掃除する
watch TV テレビを観る
get something to eat
　　　　　　　何か食べるものを手に入れる
have lunch 昼食をとる
have dinner 夕食をとる
have a date デートをする
go bowling ボウリングに行く
go dancing 踊りに行く
go fishing 釣りに行く
go hiking ハイキングに行く
go horseback riding 乗馬に行く
go shopping 買い物に行く
go for a drive ドライブに行く
go to the beach ビーチに行く
catch a movie 映画を観に行く
see a movie 映画を観る
see a play 芝居を観る
play tennis テニスをする

Adjectives

French フランスの
Italian イタリアの
Thai タイの
wonderful すてきな、素晴らしい
fantastic 素晴らしい、夢のような
great すごく良い、素晴らしい
not bad 悪くはない
okay まあまあ
all right まあまあ
interesting おもしろい
exciting わくわくする
fancy おしゃれな
beautiful 美しい
relaxing リラックスさせる
comfortable くつろいだ
quiet 穏やかな
busy 忙しい
easy 簡単な
difficult 難しい
tough きつい
tired 疲れた
dull つまらない、ありふれた
boring つまらない、うんざりする
bad 悪い、楽しくない
terrible ひどく悪い、悲惨な
uncomfortable 不快な

Adverbs and Prepositions

in front of …の前に
until …まで

33

Themes: Likes and dislikes / Food and drink
Grammar items: Expressing likes and dislikes
Speaking skills: Using polite language / Ordering in a restaurant

Building Blocks 1   Student Book: p. 36

Listen In

Answers

1. Italian food   **2.** tofu, chocolate   **3.** hamburger

Audio Scripts

1. ▶ Audio: A-53

A: What kind of food do you like?
B: I love Italian food.
A: I like Italian, too, but I prefer Indian food.
B: Really? I think Indian food is too spicy.
A: Maybe, but Indian curries are the best in the world.
B: Oh, well … how about Chinese food?
A: Personally, I don't like it very much because I find it too oily.
B: Well, I think it's very delicious.

2. ▶ Audio: A-54

A: Do you like sushi?
B: No, not at all. Sorry, but I can't stand raw fish. I love tofu, though.
A: Me, too. Everyone loves tofu. How about Japanese sweets?
B: I love any kind of sweets. Actually, I'm a chocoholic.
A: Really? I like chocolate a lot, but I couldn't eat it every day.
B: Well, I eat chocolate every day.
A: That's dangerous.

3. ▶ Audio: A-55

A: How about going out for some chicken tonight?
B: You know I hate chicken.
A: Oh, sorry, I forgot. Well, then how about going out for a hamburger?
B: That's a good idea. Hamburgers are my favorites.
A: Well, which hamburger shop shall we go to?

Speaking Strategy   Student Book: p. 37

Speak Out 1

Sample Answers

Could, Kobe beef steak, I'd like, is, where

Listen In

Answers

1. $10.00

2. $15.00

3. $14.00

4. $13.00

Audio Scripts

1. ► Audio: A-58

A: May I help you?

B: Yes. I'd like to have the lunch special, please.

A: All right. Will that be spaghetti, fish, or pizza?

B: I'll have the pizza, please.

A: Would you like soup or salad?

B: I'll have the salad with oil and vinegar dressing, please.

A: Okay. And what would you like to drink?

B: I'll have a coffee, please.

A: Is that everything, sir?

B: Yes.

A: Okay, so that'll be a pizza lunch special, a salad with oil and vinegar, and a cup of coffee.

B: That's right.

A: I'll be right back, sir.

B: Thank you.

2. ► Audio: A-59

A: Excuse me, waiter. I'd like to order.

B: Sure.

A: I'd like to have the tomato spaghetti, please.

B: Would you like soup or salad with that?

A: I'll have the onion soup, please.

B: Uh-huh. Would you like anything to drink?

A: I'd like a cola, please.

B: Okay. Is that everything?

A: Yes.

B: Good. I'll be right back with your order.

A: Thank you.

3. ► Audio: A-60

A: May I help you?

B: Yes. I'd like to have the lunch special, please.

A: Will that be spaghetti, fish, or pizza?

B: I'd like the fish, please.

A: All right. Would you like soup or salad?

B: I'll have the salad with French dressing, please.

A: Okay. And what would you like to drink?

B: I'll have coffee, please.

A: I see. Is there anything else?

B: Well … yes. Could I have the tomato soup also, please?

A: Sure. Is that everything?

B: Yeah.

A: I'll be right back with your order.

B: Thanks.

4. ► Audio: A-61

A: Can I help you?

B: Yes. I'm in a bit of a hurry. Could I have some French fries and a Ceasar salad?

A: Of course. Will that be large or small fries?

B: Small, please. And I'd like a glass of water and an espresso.

A: Fine. Is there anything else?

B: No. That's all.

A: Okay. I'll come back with your food as soon as I can.

B: I'd appreciate that.

Japanese Translations

Useful Phrases

I'm in a bit of a hurry.
ちょっと急いでいます。

I'll be right back. すぐに戻ります。
I'd appreciate that. それは助かります。
Me, too. 私も。
That's all. 以上です。
I can't stand … …が嫌いです。
At first, … 初めに、…
as soon as I can できるだけ早く
the best in the world 世界一
not at all 全く…でない

Nouns

anything 何か
everything 全部
cuisine 料理、調理法
dish 料理
fast food ファストフード、即席料理
menu メニュー
today's special 本日のお薦め料理
noodle 麺
pasta パスタ
spaghetti スパゲティ
pizza ピザ
omelet オムレツ
hamburger ハンバーガー
curry カレー
beef bowl 牛丼
raw fish 生魚
soup スープ
miso soup 味噌汁
French fries フライドポテト
Ceasar salad シーザーサラダ
dressing ドレッシング
oil and vinegar オイルとビネガー
Thousand Island サウザンドアイランド
meat sauce ミートソース
meat 肉
chicken 鶏肉

pork 豚肉
vegetable 野菜
pickles ピクルス
drink 飲み物
juice ジュース
Espresso エスプレッソ
bottled water ミネラルウォーター
wine ワイン
sweets 甘い物
chocolate チョコレート
chocoholic チョコ好き
sir [男性への呼びかけ語の] お客さま
ma'am [女性への呼びかけ語の] お客さま
chef シェフ、料理人
waiter ウエーター
waitress ウエートレス
workplace 職場
restaurant レストラン
washroom トイレ
restroom トイレ、化粧室

Verbs

practice 練習する
open 開く
close 閉まる
eat out 外食する
have *something* for breakfast
朝食に…を食べる
order 注文する
change 変える
serve 提供する
live without *something*
…なしで生きていく
prefer より好む
hate 嫌う

Adjectives

Chinese 中国の
French フランスの
Greek ギリキャの

Indian インドの
Italian イタリアの
Japanese 日本の
Korean 韓国の
Mexican メキシコの
Russian ロシアの
Spanish スペインの
Thai タイの
Vietnamese ベトナムの
vegetarian 菜食主義の
delicious とてもおいしい
better より良い
spicy 香辛料の効いた
oily 油分の多い
fried 油で揚げた
deep-fried たっぷりの油で揚げた
barbequed 丸焼きにした
steamed 蒸した
boiled 茹でた
grilled 網焼きにした
daily 毎日の
unusual 珍しい
favorite 大好きな
nearest 最も近い
polite 丁寧な
impolite 失礼な

Adverbs and Prepositions

a lot とても、すごく

Themes: The Future
Grammar items: Future tense questions and answers
Speaking skills: Agreeing and disagreeing / Expressing certainty and uncertainty

Building Blocks 1 Student Book: p. 42

Listen In

Answers

1. F (James and Atsushi are going to have some Middle Eastern food for dinner.)
2. T
3. F (The man is going to go to the beach for a barbecue.)
4. T
5. F (The speakers are not going to get married to each other.)
6. F (The man wants to have nine children.)

Audio Scripts

1. ► Audio: A-63

   A: Hey, James. What are you going to do tonight?
   B: Atsushi and I are going to go out and eat some Middle Eastern food.
   A: Can I come along?
   B: Sure.

2. ► Audio: A-64

   A: So, what will you do on the weekend?
   B: Some friends are coming over, and we're going to cook, eat, and watch movies all night.
   A: Is it all right if I join you?
   B: Sure.

3. ► Audio: A-65

   A: Where are you going after school today?
   B: I'm going to the beach and have a barbeque with some friends.
   A: Whose barbeque are you using?
   B: We're going to borrow John's.

4. ► Audio: A-66

   A: Do you have any plans for the New Year's holidays?
   B: Yeah. I'm planning to visit my friends in LA and Chicago. How about you?
   A: I'm going to travel around the eastern part of the States.
   B: That'll be interesting.

5. ► Audio: A-67

   A: So, what are you looking forward to doing when you're older?
   B: Hmm. That's a difficult question. Um … I think I'm looking forward to owning my own apartment, and … um … just taking it easy. How about you?
   A: Me? Well, I'm looking forward to getting married, and … uh … having children, I guess.

6. ► Audio: A-68

   A: How many children do you want to have?
   B: Um … well … I hope to have nine kids.
   A: Nine kids? That's a lot!
   B: I know, but my dream is to make a family baseball team. Haha.

Speak Out

Answers

1. What   2. Will   3. Who   4. are   5. looking   6. When   7. Where

Speaking Strategy   Student Book: p. 43

Speak Out 1

Sample Answers

❶ I don't think so.
❷ I agree with you.
❸ I don't think so, either.
❹ I doubt it.

Building Blocks 2   Student Book: p. 44

Listen In

Answers

1. Mike, definitely   2. sure that he's, might   3. probably, might

---

Audio Scripts

1. ▶ Audio: A-71

Mike: Hi, Sally.
Sally: Hey, Mike.
Mike: So, what are your plans for tonight?
Sally: Well, I'm probably going to finish our class homework. We have to hand it in next week.
Mike: I know, but I probably won't do it tonight. I'm so tired. I may go home early and order some pizza.
Sally: Yeah? Well, I'm kind of out of money this week, so I'll definitely cook at home. And then, I'll do the homework.

2. ▶ Audio: A-72

Mike: What are you doing tomorrow morning, Sally?
Sally: Nothing. Why?
Mike: Well, I'm definitely going jogging. Would you like to join me?
Sally: Hmm. What time are you going?
Mike: About 10 o'clock.
Sally: Okay. I might join you. It depends on how I feel in the morning.

3. ▶ Audio: A-73

Mike: Sally, are you going to take the flower arrangement class?
Sally: I'm not sure yet, but I probably won't. How about you?
Mike: I'll probably take the class. I want to study something traditional.
Sally: I see. Oh, by the way, do you know that there's a good documentary on TV tonight?
Mike: Really? What's it about?
Sally: It's about the history of geisha. I've heard it's very good. I'm definitely going to watch it.
Mike: What time is it on?
Sally: At midnight.
Mike: Midnight? Well, I'm not sure if I can watch it. I may fall asleep before midnight.
Sally: I understand.

Japanese Translations

Useful Phrases

It depends on how I feel.
気分次第です。

I've heard it's very good.
すごく良いらしい。

As for … …については
after I graduate 卒業後
before I'm 30 30歳までに
when I'm older 年をとったら、将来的に
in the future 将来
during the holidays 休暇中に
at midnight 真夜中に
for lunch 昼食に

Nouns

the sun 太陽
the moon 月
Mars 火星
century 世紀、100年
decade 10年
opinion 意見
certainty 確信、確実性
uncertainty 不安、不確実性
documentary ドキュメンタリー
Southeast Asia 東南アジア
South America 南米
fast food restaurant ファストフード店
electronics company 電子機器会社
solar battery 太陽電池
public phone 公衆電話
home phone 家の固定電話
smartphone スマートフォン
oil 石油
cost コスト、経費
environment 環境
weather 天気、気候
nature 自然
population 人口
politics 政治
whale クジラ

kid 子ども
politician 政治家
lawyer 弁護士、法律家
top model トップモデル
flower arrangement 生け花
barbeque バーベキュー
Olympic sport オリンピック種目の競技
home team 地元チーム
close game 接戦

Verbs

be sunny 晴れる
rain 雨が降る
snow 雪が降る
increase 増える
decrease 減る
be out of money 金がなくなる
run out of *something* …がなくなる
become extinct 絶滅する
become popular 人気が出る
get married to *someone* …と結婚する
have children 子どもを持っている
own a house 家を持っている
host 主催する、（主人役として）接待する
come along 同行する
join 加わる、仲間に入る
take a class 授業を受ける
fall asleep 眠り込む
pass an exam 試験に受かる
go jogging ジョギングに行く
have a plan 予定がある
plan to start *something*
…を始めるつもりだ
plan to visit *a place* …を訪れるつもりだ
plan to go to *a place* …に行くつもりだ
hope to have *something*
…を持ちたいと思っている
hope to live in *a place*
…に住みたいと思っている
hope to be *something*
…になりたいと思っている

work at a hotel ホテルで働く
work for a travel agency
旅行代理店で働く
travel with *someone* …と旅行する
travel around *a place* …を旅行する
win a game 試合に勝つ
lose a game 試合に負ける
get a ticket チケットを入手する
hand in *something* …を提出する
rent [有料で] 借りる
borrow [他者の所有物を] 借りる
agree 同意する
disagree 反対する
doubt 疑う

Adjectives

certain 確信している
sure 確信している
Middle Eastern 中東の
traditional 伝統的な
modern 現代的な
possible 可能性がある

Adverbs and Prepositions

definitely 絶対に、確かに、必ず
absolutely 絶対に、確かに、必ず
certainly 絶対に、確かに、必ず
probably おそらく
someday いつか
yet まだ
either …も（…ない）

Review for Units 4–6

Speak Out 1 Student Book: pp. 47–48

Answers

❶ had, On, for, what, going to, Sure, Where, Let's

❷ kind, love, think, so, prefer, can't stand, at all, fantastic

❸ May, like to, Will, I'll have, Would, please, what, everything, be

Listen In 1 Student Book: p. 50

Answers

1. **a)** On Sunday.

   b) Went to Asakusa, saw temples and shrines, had lunch at a tempura restaurant, saw a Kabuki play.

2. **a)** Soccer game. On Sunday.

   b) They will meet in front of the gate of the stadium at 1:30.

3. **a)** Steak.

   b) They will eat chicken at a Filipino restaurant.

4. **a)** The breakfast special: sunnyside up eggs, toast, and coffee.

   b) Espresso.

5. **a)** Four. (The man, his two friends, and the person he is talking to)

   b) In the mall.

6. **a)** He wants to jog around the Emperor's palace for the first time tomorrow morning.

   b) No.

Audio Scripts

1. ▶ Audio: A-74

   A: Hey, Pete. How was Sunday? I heard you went out with your family.

   B: It was great. We went to Asakusa and saw the temples and shrines there. It was really beautiful.

   A: And what did you do after that?

   B: We had lunch at a tempura restaurant, and then we went to see a Kabuki play.

   A: Wow. How was that?

   B: Fantastic! We used headphones, of course.

2. ▶ Audio: A-75

   A: Hi, Sophie. I have tickets for the soccer game on Sunday. Do you want to go?

   B: I'd love to. What time does the game start?

   A: It starts at 3:00 in the afternoon, so let's meet at the gate of the stadium.

   B: Okay. What time?

   A: Let me see … is 1:30 okay?

   B: 1:30 is fine. In front of the gate of the stadium.

   A: That's right. Okay, I'll see you on Sunday. Bye for now.

   B: See you.

3. ▶ Audio: A-76

A: How about going out for some steak tonight?
B: You know I hate steak.
A: Oh, sorry, I forgot. Well, then how about going out for chicken?
B: That's a good idea. There's a great Filipino restaurant that has wonderful chicken dishes.
A: Okay. Where is it?

4. ▶ Audio: A-77

A: May I help you?
B: Yes. I'd like to have the breakfast special, please.
A: Will that be eggs or pancakes?
B: I'd like the eggs, please.
A: All right. How would you like your eggs?
B: Sunnyside up.
A: Right. Would you like toast or hashed browns?
B: Toast, please.
A: What would you like to drink?
B: I'll have a coffee, please.
A: How do you want your coffee?
B: Black, please.
A: We have espresso.
B: Great. I'll have an espresso, please.
A: Is there anything else?
B: No, that's fine.
A: I'll be right back with your order.
B: Thanks.

5. ▶ Audio: A-78

A: So, what will you do on the weekend?
B: I'm going to go to a game center in the mall with two of my good friends.
A: Is that the new game center?
B: Yes.
A: Is it all right if I join you?
B: Sure.

6. ▶ Audio: A-79

A: What are you doing tomorrow morning, Sally?
B: I have no plans. Why?
A: Well, I'm definitely going to jog around the Emperor's palace for the first time. Would you like to join me?
B: The palace! Wow! That sounds great. I'd love to go. What time are you going?
A: About 7 o'clock.
B: Oooh. That's a little early for me.
A: I understand. Let's do it another time.

Listen In 2   Student Book: p. 50

Answers

1. **a)** F (The speakers will go see a movie on Sunday.)
    b) F (They will meet at 2:30 on Sunday.)
2. **a)** T
    b) F (The speakers will not go sing karaoke tonight.)
3. **a)** F (The woman doesn't like sushi.)
    b) F (The man doesn't like to eat chocolate every day.)
4. **a)** F (The woman orders spaghetti and soup.)
    b) T
5. **a)** F (The man is going to celebrate his 25th birthday with friends in Hokkaido.)
    b) T
6. **a)** T
    b) F (The man will not watch the documentary about the history of Okinawa.)

Audio Scripts

1. ▶ Audio: A-80

A: What do you want to do on the weekend?
B: I work on Saturday, so how about going to see a movie on Sunday?
A: That's a good idea. Where do you want to meet?
B: Let's meet at the McDonald's by the station.
A: Okay. What time shall we meet?
B: Is 2 o'clock okay?
A: That's too early for me. Let's make it 2:30.
B: Okay. I'll see you at the McDonald's at 2:30.

2. ▶ Audio: A-81

A: What did you do on the 18th?
B: On the 18th? I forget. Let me see … Oh yeah. After school, I studied at the café and then I had noodles with some of my friends. Then, we went to a karaoke bar.
A: Do you like karaoke?
B: Of course. How about you?
A: I love karaoke. Why don't we go singing tonight?
B: Sorry, but I can't tonight.

3. ▶ Audio: A-82

A: Do you like sushi?
B: No, not at all. Sorry, but I can't stand raw fish. I love noodles, though.
A: Me, too. Everyone loves noodles. How about Japanese sweets?
B: I love any kind of sweet. Actually, I'm a chocoholic. I eat chocolate every day.
A: Really? I like chocolate a lot, but I couldn't eat it every day.

4. ▶ Audio: A-83

A: Excuse me, waiter. I'd like to order.
B: Of course.
A: I'll have the tomato spaghetti, please.
B: Would you like soup or salad with that?
A: I'll have the onion soup, please.
B: Okay. And would you like something to drink?
A: Just a cola, please.
B: Certainly. Will there be anything else?
A: No.

5. ▶ Audio: A-84

A: Do you have any plans for your birthday?
B: Yeah. My family will have a small party for me and then I'm planning to go to Hokkaido to celebrate with my friends there.
A: That'll be great. So how old will you be?
B: It's a secret. No. I'm going to be 25.
A: Nice. So, what are you looking forward to doing when you're really old?
B: Hmm. That's a difficult question. But, I think I'm looking forward to owning my own house … and … um … just taking it easy.
A: Sounds like a good plan.

6. ▶ Audio: A-85

A: Olivia, are you going to take the tea ceremony class?
B: I'm not sure yet, but I probably won't. How about you?
A: I'll definitely take the class. I want to study something traditional.
B: I see. Oh, by the way, do you know that there's a good documentary on TV tonight?
A: Really? What's it about?
B: It's about the history of Okinawa. I'm definitely going to watch it.
A: What time is it on?
B: At midnight.
A: Midnight? Well, I'll definitely be in bed by then.

Unit 7 Travel

Themes: Travel / Directions
Grammar items: Describing location / Making comparisons
Speaking skills: Asking for and giving directions

Building Blocks 1   Student Book: p. 52

Listen In

Answers

1. e   **2.** d   **3.** f   **4.** a   **5.** g   **6.** b

Audio Scripts

1. ▶ Audio: B-03

A: Excuse me. Do you know where Victoria Park is?

B: Sure. It's down this street on the left.

A: Down this street on the left?

B: Yeah. It's just past the library. It's on the corner of Main Avenue and 3rd Street.

A: I see. Thank you.

B: You're welcome.

2. ▶ Audio: B-04

A: Excuse me. Is there a bakery near here?

B: There sure is. It's down this street on the right. It's across the street from the parking lot.

A: Okay. Thanks a lot.

B: Anytime.

3. ▶ Audio: B-05

A: Excuse me. Could you tell me where the Sky Hotel is, please?

B: Of course. It's just down this street on the right.

A: Down this street on the right?

B: That's right. It's between Joe's Pizza and the Sun Bank.

A: I think I got it. Thank you.

B: No problem.

4. ▶ Audio: B-06

A: Excuse me. Could you tell me where the City Mall is?

B: Sure. Let me see … It's down this street on the left. It's across the street from the Museum of Modern Art.

A: Okay … down this street on the left, and it's … opposite the museum?

B: That's correct.

A: I think I got it. Thank you.

B: No problem.

5. ▶ Audio: B-07

A: Excuse me. Do you know where the post office is?

B: Yeah. It's right there. It's around the corner on the left.

A: Oh. I see it. Thanks a lot.

B: My pleasure.

6. ▶ Audio: B-08

A: Excuse me. Is there a good steak restaurant near here?

B: Yup. It's called the Star Grill. It's just down this street on the left. It's the blue building next to the parking lot.

A: I appreciate your help.

B: You're welcome. Have a good day.

43

Answers

❶ Do, drugstore

❷ Is, right, on, Main, 3rd

❸ me, down, left, across, next

Speaking Strategy   Student Book: p. 53

Speak Out 1

Answers

❶ favorite

❷ prefer

❸ worst

Building Blocks 2   Student Book: p. 54

Listen In

Answers

1. h   **2.** f   **3.** g   **4.** a   **5.** d   **6.** i   **7.** c   **8.** b

---

Audio Scripts

1. ▶ Audio: B-11

A: Excuse me. Could you tell me how to get to the National Art Gallery, please?

B: Of course. Walk down this street and turn left at the first corner. You'll see it on your right.

A: So, walk down this street and turn left at the first corner?

B: That's right.

A: I think I got it. Thank you so much.

B: No problem.

2. ▶ Audio: B-12

A: Excuse me. Is there a café around here?

B: Sure. Walk past B's Mall and turn left. Then, go straight until you come to Park Drive. It's on the corner of 5th Street and Park Drive on the right side.

A: Let's see. Walk past B's Mall, turn left and then go straight. It's on the corner of 5th Street and Park Drive?

B: That's correct. It's called the Seaside Café. It's across the street from the theater.

A: I see. I appreciate your help.

B: Anytime.

3. ▶ Audio: B-13

A: Excuse me. How can I get to the Traveler's Center from here?

B: It's easy. Go straight until the very end and turn right. It's next to the Diamond Hotel.

A: Okay. Thank you for your help.

B: You're welcome. Have a good day.

A: You, too.

4. ▶ Audio: B-14

A: Excuse me. Could you tell me where the Pacific Aquarium is, please?

B: Sure. Walk down this street and turn left at the first light. Then, go straight and turn right at Park Drive.

A: Okay.

B: Then, keep walking and cross 5th and 6th Streets. It's just past the Civic Tower on your left.

A: Well, let me repeat that. First, turn left at the first light and turn right at Park Drive. Then, cross 5th and 6th Streets?

B: That's right. The aquarium is on your left.

A: I appreciate that.

B: No problem. Have a good day.

5. ▶ Audio: B-15

A: Excuse me. Could you tell me how to get to the Fisherman's Market?

B: Of course. First, go straight and turn left at 5th Street. Then, turn right at the first light and turn right at the next street. The market is at the very end of the street.

A: So, turn left at 5th Street and turn right at the first light. Then, turn right at the next street?

B: Yeah. The market is at the very end of the street.

A: I think I got it. Thank you so much.

B: No problem. Have a good day.

A: You, too.

6. ▶ Audio: B-16

A: Excuse me. Do you know where the Grand Hotel is?

B: Um … let me see. The easiest way is to just go through the park until you come to 4th Street. Go out the park and turn left. It's the first building on your left.

A: Okay. Go through the park and turn left?

B: That's correct.

A: Thank you so much.

B: Anytime. Have a good day.

A: You, too.

7. ▶ Audio: B-17

A: Excuse me. How can I get to the Union Botanical Garden from here?

B: Let me see. First, walk down this street until you come to the very end and turn left. Then, turn right at the first corner. Keep walking for about five minutes and you'll see it on your right.

A: Wow. That's complicated. First, walk until the very end and turn left. Then, turn right at the first corner and go straight for about five minutes?

B: Right. It's just past the parking lot on your right.

A: I think I got it. Thank you for your help.

B: You're welcome.

8. ▶ Audio: B-18

A: Excuse me. Is there a good restaurant near here?

B: Yeah, there are some. Um … do you like Italian food?

A: Yes, very much.

B: Okay. I'll tell you one of my favorites.

A: That's great.

B: It's called Dolphins. First, walk down this street and turn left at the second corner. Then, turn right at the first light and go straight for about three minutes. Cross 6th Street and you'll see it on your left.

A: So, I turn left at the second corner and turn right at the first light. Then, walk down and cross 6th Street?

B: That's right. Dolphins is on your left. It's between Rainbow Books and Coast Inn.

A: I see.

B: Oh, by the way, my favorite is their seafood pasta. You should try it.

A: I will.

B: Have a good day.

A: You, too. Thanks.

Sample Answers

1. Walk down this street and turn right at the first corner. You'll see it on your left.

2. Sure. Walk down this street and turn left at the first corner. Then, go straight until you come to Park Drive. It's on the corner of 4th Street and Park Drive on the right side.

3. Walk down this street and turn left at the second light. Then, go straight until you come to Union Road. It's on the corner of 5th Street and Union Road on the right side.

4. Walk down this street and turn left at the second light. Then, turn right at the first corner. You'll see it on your right. It's next to a hotel.

5. Yes. Walk down this street and turn left at the second light. Then, go straight until you come to Park Drive. It's on the corner of 5th Street and Park Drive on the left side.

6. Sure. Walk down this street and turn left at the second light. Then, turn right at the second corner. You'll see it on your left.

7. Yes. Walk down this street and turn left at the first light. Then, turn right at the first corner and go straight. Keep walking. Soon after you cross 6th Street, you'll see it on your right.

8. Walk down this street and turn left at the first light. Then, turn right at the first corner and go straight until you come to 6th Street. It's on the corner of 6th Street and Park Drive on the left side.

9. Yes. Walk down this street and turn left at the second light. Then, turn right at the first corner and go straight. You'll see it on your right. It's just past the bus terminal.

10. Sure. Walk down this street and turn left at the second light. Then, turn right at the first corner. You'll see it on your left. It's next to a theater.

Japanese Translations

Useful Phrases

Excuse me. すみません。
There sure is. もちろんあります。
Let's see. ええと。
Let me see. ええと。
Let me repeat that. 繰り返してみます。
That's correct. その通りです。
That's right. その通りです。
Right. そうです。
Yup. ええ。
I see. わかりました。
I think I got it. わかったと思います。
Thanks a lot. どうもありがとう。
You're welcome. どういたしまして。
My pleasure. どういたしまして。
No problem. いえいえ。
Anytime. いえいえ。
You, too. あなたも。
The easiest way is …
　　　　　　　　　一番簡単な方法は…です。
It's called … …という名称です。
on the left 左に
on your right あなたの右側に
across the street from …
　　　　　　　　　　　…の向かいに
on the other side of … …の反対側に
on the corner of … and …
　　　　　　　　　…と…が交わる角に
around the corner 角を曲がったところに
at the very end of the street
　　　　　　　　　通りの突き当たりに
more interesting より興味深い
the most interesting 最も興味深い
the best 最高の
the worst 最悪の

Nouns

map 地図
tower 塔
light 信号

avenue 通り
road 道路
drive 通り
embassy 大使館
city hall 市庁舎、市役所
police station 警察署
post office 郵便局
bank 銀行
bus terminal バスターミナル
parking lot 駐車場
park 公園
aquarium 水族館
botanical garden 植物園
museum 美術館、博物館
gallery 画廊、美術館
music center 音楽堂
theater 劇場、映画館
bookstore 書店
drugstore ドラッグストア
jewelry store 宝石店
travel agency 旅行代理店
traveler's center 観光案内所
hotel ホテル
inn ［比較的安価な］ホテル、宿
mall ショッピングモール、商店街
market 市場
mart 小売店
bakery パン屋
coffee shop 喫茶店
café カフェ
kitchen 食堂、軽食レストラン
diner 食堂、軽食レストラン
bistro 小レストラン、居酒屋
grill 料理店、バーベキュー店
steak restaurant ステーキハウス
seafood シーフード、海鮮物
ocean 海
iceberg 氷山
science 科学
natural history 自然史

Verbs

give directions 道順を教える
walk down 歩いて行く
go straight まっすぐ進む
go through 通り抜ける
keep walking 歩き続ける
turn 曲がる
cross 横断する、渡る
come to *a place* …まで到達する
get to *a place* …に行く
go out *a place* …から出る
have a great time 楽しい時間を過ごす
decide 決める

Adjectives

favorite 大好きな
complicated 複雑な、ややこしい
tasty おいしい

Adverbs and Prepositions

next to …の隣に
between …の間に
opposite …の向かい側に
in front of …の前に
behind …の裏に
past …を過ぎて
right there ちょうどそこに
politely 丁寧に

Themes: Entertainment
Grammar items: Asking for and giving information
Speaking skills: Asking for repetition

Building Blocks 1 Student Book: p. 58

Listen In

Answers

1. 7:20, 9:45, 1
2. open, 9:30, Thursdays, 15, over
3. every, 8:00
4. 28, 15, 12, under

Audio Scripts

1. ► Audio: B-20

   A: Century Cinema. May I help you?
   B: Yes. Could you tell me what time *Star Wars 15* is playing in the evening?
   A: Sure. It starts at 7:20 and 9:45.
   B: I see. Is there a late show tonight?
   A: Yes, there is. It starts at 1 o'clock.
   B: Okay. Thank you very much.
   A: You're welcome. Have a good day.

2. ► Audio: B-21

   A: National Animal Park. Can I help you?
   B: Hi. I'd like to know your opening and closing times, please.
   A: Sure. We're open from 10:00 a.m. until 9:30 p.m., and we're closed on Thursdays.
   B: I see. And I'd like to know how much the tickets cost, please.
   A: It costs 15 dollars for adults and children, and 10 dollars for seniors over the age of 60.
   B: Okay. Thank you so much.
   A: My pleasure.

3. ► Audio: B-22

   A: Sam's Music. Jim speaking.
   B: Hi. Could you tell me your opening hours, please?
   A: Sure. We open at 10:30 every morning and close at 8:00 at night.
   B: I'm sorry but what time was that again?
   A: We open at 10:30 and close at 8:00.
   B: I got it. Thank you.
   A: Anytime.

4. ► Audio: B-23

   A: Wonderland Amusement Park. May I help you?
   B: Hi. I'd like to know how much the tickets cost, please.
   A: Okay. Um … it costs 28 dollars for adults and 15 dollars for children under the age of 12.
   B: I'm sorry but could you repeat that, please?
   A: Sure. Twenty-eight dollars for adults and 15 dollars for children under the age of 12. Oh … and I forgot. It's free for children under the age of five.
   B: Got it. Thank you very much.
   A: You're welcome.

Speak Out 1

Sample Answers

❶ Could you say that again, please?

❷ Could you repeat that, please?, Sorry, but how much was that again?

Building Blocks 2   Student Book: p. 60

Listen In

Answers

1. F (The man recommends that the woman see the move because it is exciting.)
2. T
3. F (The man likes the amusement park because there are a lot of things to do there.)
4. F (The woman thinks the man should read Stephen King's novels.)
5. T

Audio Scripts

1. ▶ Audio: B-26

   A: What kind of movies do you like?
   B: I love action movies.
   A: Did you see Pat Brad's new movie?
   B: Yeah. It was good. I definitely think you should see it because it's so exciting. It's one of the best action movies I've seen.

2. ▶ Audio: B-27

   A: How's the new book that you're reading?
   B: It's not very good. The story is too complicated. I've read her other books and they were very good.
   A: Okay. I'll read one of her earlier books.

3. ▶ Audio: B-28

   A: Hey Jimmy. How was the amusement park that you went to on the weekend?
   B: It was great. There are a lot of things to do there.
   A: That sounds fun.
   B: If you have time, you should go there. The rides are a little bit expensive, though.

4. ▶ Audio: B-29

   A: Have you ever read the comic *Living Dead*?
   B: No. What kind of comic is it?
   A: It's a horror story about zombies. I read it the other day and it was so dull.
   B: That's too bad. Well, I recommend that you read Stephen King's novels. They're very scary.

5. ▶ Audio: B-30

   A: Do you like playing video games?
   B: Yeah, very much.
   A: What was the last game that you played?
   B: It was a new role-playing game called "Ghostblazer."
   A: Would you recommend it?
   B: No. I don't recommend it because the story is boring.
   A: Oh, I see.

Japanese Translations

Useful Phrases

Can I help you? ご用件を承ります。
Jim speaking. ［電話の応答で］ジムです。
Got it. わかりました。
That sounds fun. おもしろそうですね。
I like many kinds. 何でも好きです。
I like it a lot. 大好きです。
Not very much. そうでもありません。
It's free for … …には無料です。
the last movie that you saw
　　　　　　　あなたが一番最近観た映画
as many … as you can
　　　　　　　できるだけたくさんの…
the other day ついこの間
under the age of 12 12歳未満の
over the age of 60 60歳以上の
on the computer パソコンで

Nouns

entertainment 娯楽、エンタメ
animal park 自然動物園
information 情報
opening hours 営業時間
opening time 始業時刻
closing time 終業時刻
afternoon show 午後の上演
evening show 夜の上演
late show 深夜の上演
ride 乗り物
ticket チケット、券
Euro ユーロ
adult 大人
senior 高齢者
music 音楽
sound 音、サウンド
pop ポップ
rock ロック
jazz ジャズ
hip hop ヒップホップ
gospel ゴスペル

singer 歌手
voice 声
TV program テレビ番組
game show ゲーム番組、クイズ番組
talk show トークショー、対談番組
sports スポーツ
pro wrestling プロレス
film 映画
story ストーリー、話
special effects 特撮、特殊効果
acting 演技
action movie アクション映画
animation アニメーション、アニメ
drama ドラマ
suspense サスペンス
thriller スリラー、恐怖
musical ミュージカル
science fiction SF
fantasy ファンタジー
adventure アドベンチャー、冒険
comedy コメディ、喜劇
romance ロマンス、恋愛
mystery ミステリー、推理
novel 小説
comic book 漫画本
video game テレビゲーム
role-playing game
　　　　　　ロールプレーイングゲーム
card game トランプゲーム、カードゲーム
board game ボードゲーム
racing game レースゲーム
fighting game 格闘ゲーム
puzzle game パズルゲーム
repetition 繰り返し
recommendation お薦め、提案
living dead ゾンビ
zombie ゾンビ

Verbs

be sure about *something*
　　　　　　　…を確認する

play 上演する、［ゲームを］する
watch ［テレビ番組を］観る
enter 入場する、入る
start 始まる、開始する
turn up the volume 音量を上げる
keep *something* going …を続ける
recommend 薦める、提案する

Adjectives

classical クラシックの
powerful 力強い、迫力のある
funny 笑える
cool すごい、いけてる
scary 怖い
horror 恐怖の
other 他の
earlier 以前の、初期の

Adverbs and Prepositions

ever 今までに
almost ほぼ、ほとんど
a little bit 少しだけ、ちょっとだけ
though …だけど

Themes: Health and exercise
Grammar items: Describing routines / Giving instructions
Speaking skills: Using numbers

Building Blocks 1 Student Book: p. 64

Listen In

Answers

1. [1] get up at 6 a.m. [4] work out in the gym [2] go for a run [5] check e-mail [3] have breakfast
2. [4] play a few games [6] finish around 7 p.m. [3] practice shots [1] do stretching exercises [5] clean the courts [2] hit the balls around
3. [3] take a shower [6] have classes [2] walk the dog [1] wake up around 10 a.m. [5] have lunch [7] study or work part-time [4] ride bicycle to school

---

Audio Scripts

1. ▶ Audio: B-32

A: So, David, you're now working as a professional athlete, right?

B: Yeah.

A: Do you exercise every day?

B: Well, to be honest, I'm quite strict about my exercise and diet routine.

A: I see. What's your morning routine?

B: I get up early … um … usually at 6 a.m. First, I go for a run in the park and then I have fruit and juice for breakfast. After that, I work out in my home gym. Finally, I check my e-mail before lunch. That's a typical morning for me.

A: Sounds tiring to me, but that's why you're in great shape.

2. ▶ Audio: B-33

A: Rachel, what's the usual routine for the tennis club?

B: Well, first, we do some stretching exercises. After that, we hit the balls around and then practice certain shots and things like that. Then, we play a few games. Finally, we clean the courts and finish around 7 p.m.

A: I'm very interested in joining the tennis club. I'm not very good, though.

B: Don't worry. You can do it.

3. ▶ Audio: B-34

A: What's your typical day like?

B: Well, I'm not a morning person, so I usually wake up around 10 a.m. or so. After that, I walk my dog and then take a shower. Then, I ride my bicycle to school and have lunch with my friends.

A: What about breakfast?

B: I always skip it.

A: I see. What do you do in the afternoon and evening then?

B: I have classes in the afternoon. After school, I study or work part-time.

A: Sounds like you're busy.

Speak Out 1

Sample Answers

In the morning

First, Takako gets up at 5:30 a.m.

After that, she eats a light breakfast.

Next, she runs 15 km and then does stretching exercises.

Then, she takes a shower.

Finally, she meets with her manager.

In the afternoon and evening

First, Takako has lunch.

After that, she works out at a gym and then take a shower.

Next, she cooks dinner.

Then, she watches TV.

Finally, she goes to bed around 10 p.m.

Speaking Strategy   Student Book: p. 65

Speak Out 1

Answers

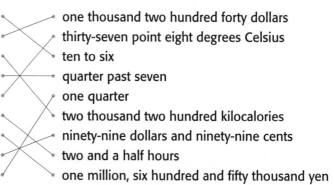

1. Tom usually wakes up at **5:50**.
2. Linda paid **$1,240** to her sports club last year.
3. He needs to take in **2,200 kcal** per day.
4. I left home for jogging at **7:15**.
5. My temperature was about **37.8°C** last night.
6. I work out for **2.5 hours** every weekend.
7. My family spent **¥1,650,000** on groceries last year.
8. Bob bought a suit and it was **$99.99**.
9. I used **1/4** of a package of tofu for the miso soup.

- one thousand two hundred forty dollars
- thirty-seven point eight degrees Celsius
- ten to six
- quarter past seven
- one quarter
- two thousand two hundred kilocalories
- ninety-nine dollars and ninety-nine cents
- two and a half hours
- one million, six hundred and fifty thousand yen

Listen In

Answers

1. ☐3 Put all the ingredients into a blender and mix.   ☐5 Enjoy the Blueberry Tofu Wonder.
   ☐2 Cut up the banana.   ☐1 Prepare the ingredients.   ☐4 Pour the juice into a glass.
2. ☐6 Put the bananas into a blender.   ☐8 Turn on the blender and mix.   ☐5 Slice up the other banana.
   ☐2 Cut up one banana.   ☐3 Put the banana into the freezer.   ☐1 Prepare the ingredients.
   ☐7 Add ice cubes, yogurt, and water.   ☐4 Take out the frozen banana after an hour.

Audio Scripts

1. ▶ Audio: B-37

Today, I'm going to tell you how to make the Blueberry Tofu Wonder. If you're interested in staying healthy or losing weight, this is the perfect drink for you. The ingredients are simple. First, you need one cup of frozen blueberries, one banana, a half package of tofu, one cup of water, and a tablespoon of honey. Next, cut up the banana. Then, put all the ingredients into a blender and mix. After that, pour the juice into a glass. Finally, enjoy your Blueberry Tofu Wonder.

2. ▶ Audio: B-38

Now, I'm going to tell you how to make a healthy drink called the Frozen Banana Special. It'll give you lots of energy and it's very good for you. First, prepare two bananas, a cup of yogurt, a few ice cubes, and a cup of water. Next, cut up one banana and put it into the freezer. Then, after an hour, take out the frozen banana and slice up the other banana. After that, put them into a blender. Finally, add ice cubes, yogurt, and water, and then turn on the blender and mix.

Speak Out

Answers

2. oil, juice
4. cucumbers
5. lettuce

Japanese Translations

Useful Phrases

It sounds healthy. 健康的ですね。
You can do it. あなたならできますよ。
I'm supposed to …
                …することになっています。
I get accustomed to …
                …に慣れています。
ten to six 6時10分前、5時50分
five past seven 7時5分
half an hour 30分、半時間
a half package of tofu 豆腐半丁
one third of a cup 3分の1カップ
one slice of bread パン1枚
a tablespoon of honey
                大さじ1杯のハチミツ
36 degrees Celsius 摂氏36度
for my health 健康のために
on weekdays 平日に
right now 今すぐに
per day 1日あたり
at least 少なくとも
on top 一番上に
to be honest 実は、本音を言うと

Nouns

population 人口
average body temperature 平熱
energy エネルギー
diet 食事
routine 習慣
morning person 早起き、朝型（の人）
athlete 競技者、アスリート
full marathon フルマラソン
home gym 自宅のトレーニングルーム
court [テニスの] コート
yoga mattress ヨガ用マットレス
sweat suit スウェットスーツ
medicine 薬
light breakfast 軽めの朝食
food supply 食料供給

groceries 食料品
recipe 調理法、レシピ
ingredient 材料
mixture 混ぜ合わせたもの
shellfish 貝
lettuce レタス
celery セロリ
blueberry ブルーベリー
peanut butter ピーナッツバター
plain yogurt プレーンヨーグルト
power drink 栄養ドリンク
soy milk 豆乳
ice cube [冷凍庫で作る立方体の] 氷
freezer 冷凍庫
blender ミキサー
bowl ボウル
plate 平皿

Verbs

be careful about *something*
                …に気をつける
be in great shape
                体調が良い、とても元気である
stay healthy 健康を保つ
weigh …の重さがある
gain weight 太る、体重が増える
lose weight 痩せる、減量する
take in 1,800 kilocalories
                1800キロカロリーを摂取する
go for a run ひとっ走りする
walk a dog 犬の散歩をする
take a sauna サウナに入る
cool down 体を冷やす
take a nap 仮眠をとる
skip breakfast 朝食を抜く
check e-mail メールチェックをする
leave home 家を出る
arrive in class 教室に着く
practice *something* …の練習をする
do a push-up 腕立て伏せをする
do a sit-up 腹筋をする

do stretching exercises 柔軟体操をする
do weight training
                ウエートトレーニングをする
hit balls around ボールを打ち合う
give instructions 指示を出す、説明する
describe [言葉で] 説明する
prepare 用意する、準備する
take out *something* …を取り出す
cut up 切る
cut *something* into thin slices
                …を薄切りにする
slice up 薄切りにする、薄く切る
add 加える
pour 注ぐ
mix 混ぜ合わせる
put [容器に] 入れる、[上に] 乗せる
match 照合する、マッチさせる

Adjectives

professional プロの
amateur アマチュアの
perfect 完璧な、理想的な
ideal 最良の、理想的な
typical 典型的な
long-distance 長距離の
tiring きつい、疲れる
fresh 新鮮な、出来立ての
frozen 凍った、冷凍の

Adverbs and Prepositions

extremely とっても、極めて
easily 簡単に、たやすく

Review for Units 7–9

Speak Out 1   Student Book: pp. 69–70

Answers

❶ Excuse, Could, course, down, right, between, Where, near, across, problem

❷ kind, fantasy, want, I'll, May, Could, what time, Sure, Thank

❸ How's, pretty, about, what's, get up, First, and then, After that, Finally, typical

Listen In 1   Student Book: p. 72

Answers

1. **a)** It's down the street on the left. [It's on the corner of Main Avenue and 3rd Street.]
   b) It's down the street on the right. [It's across the street from Victoria Park.]
2. **a)** Main Street.
   b) The Civic Tower.
3. **a)** 10:30 in the morning and 6:00 at night.
   b) 10:30 in the morning and 8:00 at night.
4. **a)** It's about 2,500 meters and it takes about 15 minutes.
   b) Around 130 kilometers per hour.
5. **a)** Warm-up exercises, sing a few songs, and practice for the next concert.
   b) Every Thursday and Friday from 4 to 7.
6. **a)** One avocado, two cups of milk, vanilla, maple syrup, and salt.
   b) The avocado and the milk.

Audio Scripts

1. ► Audio: B-39

A: Excuse me. Do you know where Victoria Park is?
B: Sure. It's down this street on the left.
A: Down this street on the left?
B: Yeah. It's on the corner of Main Avenue and 3rd Street.
A: One more thing. Is there a bakery near here?
B: There sure is. It's down this same street on the right. It's across the street from Victoria Park.
A: Okay. Thanks a lot.
B: Anytime.

2. ► Audio: B-40

A: Excuse me. Could you tell me where the National Art Museum is, please?
B: Sure. It's on Main Street. Just walk down this street and turn left at the first corner. That's Main Street. Then, keep walking and the art museum is on your left just past the Civic Tower.
A: Well, let me repeat that. First, walk down here and turn left at Main Street. Keep walking and it's on the left?
B: That's right. It's just past the Civic Tower.
A: Thank you. I appreciate that.
B: No problem. Have a good day.
A: You, too.

3. ▶ Audio: B-41

A: Sam's Music. Jim speaking.

B: Hi. Could you tell me your opening hours, please?

A: Sure. We open at 10:30 every morning and close at 6:00 at night.

B: Is that the same for the weekend?

A: No. We open at the same time, but we close at 8:00 on the weekends.

B: I got it. Thank you.

A: Anytime.

4. ▶ Audio: B-42

A: Hey Jimmy. How was the amusement park that you went to on the weekend?

B: It was great. There are a lot of things to do there.

A: How was the roller coaster?

B: Fantastic. It's about 2,500 meters long and it takes about 15 minutes.

A: Cool. How high does it go?

B: About 80 meters high and it travels at around 130 kilometers per hour.

A: Wow!

5. ▶ Audio: B-43

A: Rachel, what's the usual routine for the singing club?

B: Well, first, we do some warm-up exercises. After that, we sing a few songs, and then we practice for the next concert.

A: What time do you usually meet?

B: We meet every Thursday and Friday from 4 to 7.

A: I'm thinking of joining the club. When is the next concert?

B: On July 5th.

6. ▶ Audio: B-44

Now, I'm going to tell you how to make an avocado smoothie. First, let's look at the ingredients. You will need one avocado, two cups of milk, some vanilla, maple syrup, and some salt. Now, here's what you need to do. First, cut the avocado and put it and the milk into a blender. Add just a little vanilla and maple syrup, about 1 teaspoon, and then a pinch of salt. Finally, turn on the blender and mix. It's a delicious and healthy drink.

(**Listen In 2**)   Student Book: p. 72

Answers

1. **a)** T
   b) F (The restaurant is not close to the post office. *The man telling the directions says, "It's quite far, about a 25-minute walk."*)

2. **a)** F (The Grand Hotel is not in the park. *The man says, "Go out the park."*)
   b) F (The hotel is a big blue building.)

3. **a)** T
   b) F (Children under five get in free.)

4. **a)** T
   b) T

5. **a)** F (The man wakes up and then walks his dog.)
   b) T

6. **a)** F (The ingredients for this drink are orange juice, 1 cup of strawberries, one banana, honey and ice cubes.)
   b) F (You can drink it anytime during the day.)

Audio Scripts

1. ▶ Audio: B-45

A: Excuse me. Do you know where the post office is?

B: Yeah. It's right there on the corner.

A: Oh. I see it. And one more thing. Is there a good steak restaurant near here?

B: Yup. It's called the Star Grill. It's quite far, about a 25-minute walk.

A: I don't mind.

B: Just keep walking down this street. It'll be on your right side, just past the big park.

A: I appreciate your help.

B: You're welcome. Have a good day.

2. ▶ Audio: B-46

A: Excuse me. Do you know where the Grand Hotel is?

B: Um … let me see. The easiest way is to just go through the park until you come to Green Drive. Go out the park and turn right. It's the first building on your left.

A: Okay. Go through the park and turn left?

B: No. Turn right and then it's on your left. It's a big blue building. You can't miss it.

A: I got it. Thanks.

B: Anytime.

3. ▶ Audio: B-47

A: Dream World Amusement Park. How can I help you?

B: Hi. I'd like to know how much the tickets cost, please.

A: Okay. Um … it costs 28 dollars for adults and 15 dollars for children under the age of 16.

B: Okay, thanks.

A: Oh … and I forgot. It's free for children under the age of five.

B: Got it. Thank you very much.

A: You're welcome.

4. ▶ Audio: B-48

A: Do you like watching anime?

B: Yeah, very much.

A: What kind do you like?

B: Well, I like monster and zombie anime the best.

A: Interesting. I prefer anime with princes and princesses.

B: I like that kind also, but I don't watch them very much. I like lots of blood.

A: So, what recent anime would you recommend?

B: Let's see. There's a new one called, *Zoombies.*

A: Oh, I've seen it. It's very violent.

B: Maybe, but the story is fantastic!

5. ▶ Audio: B-49

A: What's your typical day like?

B: Well, I'm not a morning person, so I usually wake up around 7 a.m. or so. After that, I walk my dog and then take a shower. Then, I ride my bicycle to school, have a few classes, and have lunch with my friends.

A: What about breakfast?

B: I always skip it.

A: I see. What do you do in the afternoon and evening then?

B: I have classes in the afternoon. After school, I have tennis practice.

A: Sounds like you're busy.

6. ▶ Audio: B-50

Now, I'm going to tell you how to make a healthy energy smoothie. For this, you will need a cup of orange juice, one cup of strawberries, one banana, some honey and some ice cubes. Put all this in a blender and mix. It's a great drink for breakfast but you can drink it anytime during the day.

Themes: Describing people
Grammar items: Emphasizing adjectives
Speaking skills: Describing people's physical looks / Describing personality

Building Blocks 1 Student Book: p. 74

Listen In

Answers

Audio Scripts

1. ▶ Audio: B-52

A: It's a great party, isn't it?
B: Yes, it is.
A: Hey, look! There's Richard Brown. He's on the soccer team. He's so cute.
B: Where? I don't see him. Which one?
A: He's really tall and has short dark hair. He's wearing a red sweater.
B: Oh, yeah, I see him.
A: He's so athletic … and he's really cool.
B: Do you think so?

2. ▶ Audio: B-53

A: There's Richard Brown's girlfriend over there.
B: Oh, no! Don't tell me he has a girlfriend.
A: Yes, unfortunately. She has long blonde hair. She's wearing a blue dress.
B: She's pretty.
A: Yeah. She's the head cheerleader.

3. ▶ Audio: B-54

A: Hey, look over there. That's my science teacher. He's my favorite teacher. He's not so handsome, but he is smart and funny. I like him a lot.
B: Which one is he?
A: He's bald and wears glasses. He's standing alone.
B: Well, I hope he's my science teacher next year.

4. ▶ Audio: B-55

A: Look! Theresa Bart is here, too. Do you know her?
B: No. I don't.
A: She's by the window. She's kind of chubby and has long straight hair.
B: Is she wearing a polka-dot dress?
A: That's right.

5. ▶ Audio: B-56

A: Wow. Al Brown is here, too. He's Richard Brown's brother.

B: Really? Which one is he?

A: He's talking with Richard's girlfriend. He's kind of short and muscular. He has a shaved head.

B: I see him. What does he do?

A: He plays rugby.

6. ▶ Audio: B-57

A: Hey, who's that good-looking guy?

B: Which one?

A: There's a tall guy over there. He has short red hair and he's really thin.

B: Oh, that's Mike Winward. He's the drummer in the school band.

A: Really? Please introduce him to me.

Building Blocks 2 Student Book: p. 76

Listen In

Answers

1. nice, interesting, more, outgoing
2. shy, smartest, negative, more, funnier
3. quietest, kind, rude, selfish, funny, friendly, good-looking

---

Audio Scripts

1. ▶ Audio: B-60

A: What do you think of our class so far?

B: I really like it. We have some interesting classmates.

A: What do you think of Dave?

B: He's nice. I talked with him last night and he's very interesting. He knows a lot about music.

A: I didn't know that. I like him because he's more energetic and outgoing than the other guys in class.

B: Yeah, he's a lot of fun.

2. ▶ Audio: B-61

A: Hey, do you know anything about Alice?

B: Yeah, a lot. I like her.

A: What's she like?

B: She's kind of shy, but she's really smart. In fact, she's the smartest girl in class. Did you know that she had the highest grades last year?

A: Really? That's fantastic.

B: You know, I also like the exchange student Linda. She was kind of negative at the beginning, but now she's more positive. And she's funnier than Alice.

A: She makes me laugh a lot.

3. ▶ Audio: B-62

A: Did you know that Takako and Kim are best friends?

B: I know. Kim is the quietest student in class, but I like her. She's extremely kind.

A: I like her, too. But, … did you know that she and Paul share the same apartment?

B: You're kidding! I'm sorry but I don't like him at all. He's very rude.

A: And so selfish.

B: Yeah. It's difficult to believe that Mark is his brother because he's definitely different. Mark is so funny and friendly.

A: I know. He's a lot of fun.

B: And he's really good-looking.

A: You sound like you like him.

B: I do! I wish I could go out with him!

Japanese Translations

Useful Phrases

Which one? どの人?

He's just like you.
彼はあなたにそっくりですね。

She's a lot of fun.
彼女はすごくおもしろいよ。

I wish I could … …できるといいな。

when necessary 必要な場合は

at the beginning 最初は

by the window 窓際に

over there あそこに

Nouns

rugby ラグビー

school band 学校のバンド

head cheerleader
チアリーダーのキャプテン

exchange student 交換留学生

guy 男の子、男子

shaved head 坊主頭、スキンヘッド

beard あごひげ

moustache 口ひげ

clothes 服装、服

jacket ジャケット、上着

sweater セーター

shirt シャツ

skirt スカート

jeans ジーンズ

glasses 眼鏡

personality 人柄、性格

grade 成績

Verbs

be out of shape かっこ悪い

be best friends 親友になる

get along with *someone*
…と気が合う、…と仲良くする

make *someone* laugh …を笑わせる

stand alone [人から離れて] 一人で立つ

wear 身に着けている

share シェアする、共有する

emphasize 強調する

Adjectives

short 短い、ショートの、背が低い

average height 平均身長

tall 背が高い

thin 痩せた

fit [健康的に] スラリとした

average build 中肉中背

athletic がっしりした、たくましい

muscular 筋骨隆々の、たくましい

chubby ぽっちゃりした

fat 太った

overweight 太り過ぎの

medium-length
ミディアムの、肩まで届く長さの

long ロングの、長い

straight ストレートの、まっすぐな

curly カールの、巻いた

dark 黒い、黒髪の

blonde ブロンドの、金髪の

gray 白髪 (まじり) の

bald はげた

cute かわいい

pretty かわいらしい、きれいな

beautiful 美しい、きれいな

good-looking 容姿端麗な、ハンサムな

handsome ハンサムな、顔立ちのいい

cool カッコいい、凛々しい

fashionable おしゃれな

nice [性格が] 良い、すてきな

energetic エネルギッシュな、活発な

positive 前向きな、積極的な

negative マイナス思考の、消極的な

supportive 面倒見がいい、協力的な

kind 親切な、優しい

friendly 友好的な、人なつっこい

mean 意地悪な、嫌な

outgoing 社交的な

shy 内気な、恥ずかしがりの

talkative 話し好きな、おしゃべりな

quiet 物静かな、無口な、穏やかな

hardworking 努力家の、勤勉な

lazy 怠惰な、だらしない

polite 礼儀正しい

impolite 失礼な、無礼な

rude 失礼な、無礼な

interesting おもしろい

boring つまらない、退屈な

strict 厳しい、厳格な

serious まじめな

easygoing 大らかな、のんきな

funny ユーモアがある、おかしい、変な

dull つまらない、退屈な

smart 頭の良い、賢い

stupid 頭の悪い、ばかな

sick 具合が悪い、体調が悪い

polka-dot 水玉模様の

Adverbs and Prepositions

extremely すごく、めちゃくちゃ

very すごく、とても

really すごく、本当に

kind of わりと、どちらかと言えば

sort of わりと、どちらかと言えば

not very … あまり…でない

not so … そんなに…でない

not … at all 全然…でない

Themes: Storytelling
Grammar items: Past tense questions and answers
Speaking skills: Telling stories / Reacting to events

Building Blocks 1   Student Book: p. 80

Listen In

Answers

1. T
2. T
3. F (The woman broke her phone and hurt her eye.)
4. F (The man didn't hit the deer. He tried to stop and went off the road.)
5. F (Two dogs ran after the woman and tried to bite her. The man says, "I'm glad that they didn't bite you.")

Audio Scripts

1. ▶ Audio: B-64

A: Did I tell you what happened today?
B: No. What happened?
A: While we were taking a listening test, the teacher hit the computer and knocked it over.
B: No kidding. What happened then?
A: Because the computer was broken, she had to cancel the test.
B: Wow. You were so lucky!

2. ▶ Audio: B-65

A: Did I tell you the good news?
B: No, what is it?
A: Well, … guess what. I got married last week!
B: You're kidding! How did that happen?
A: While Jenny and I were traveling in Las Vegas, we felt like getting married there.
B: I can't believe it! Well … anyway, congratulations.

3. ▶ Audio: B-66

A: What happened to your eye?
B: Oh, it was terrible.
A: What happened?
B: Um … I was walking down the street and looking at my phone and then I ran into a pole.

A: Really? That's not good.
B: No, it isn't. I hit my eye and I also broke my phone.
A: Wow! You have to be careful. And don't check your phone while you're walking.
B: I won't anymore.

4. ▶ Audio: B-67

A: Did I tell you what happened on Sunday?
B: No.
A: Well, I went for a drive and while I was driving through the mountains, I saw two deer walking across the road.
B: What happened then?
A: I didn't want to hit them, so I tried to stop and went off the road.
B: Wow! Was there any damage to your car?
A: Luckily, no! And the deer ran away safely, too.

5. ▶ Audio: B-68

A: Did I tell you about last night?
B: No. What happened?
A: While I was walking home, two dogs started following me. I started to run, but they chased me and tried to bite me.
B: That's terrible. Were you scared?
A: Of course. It was scary. I finally yelled at them, and they ran away.
B: I'm glad that they didn't bite you.

Speak Out

Answers

1. saw, fell, was washing
2. dropped, lost, was riding
3. bit, were walking
4. scratched, was sleeping
5. was doing, broke
6. went, were cleaning, found
7. were taking, rang, got
8. was studying, came, left

Speaking Strategy   Student Book: p. 81

Speak Out 1

Answers

disappointed, shocking, pleased, exciting, surprised, scared, disappointing

Building Blocks 2   Student Book: p. 82

Listen In

Answers

1. 7, found, throwing, hit, got, days
2. mom, came, asked, whole, didn't, have dinner, became

Audio Scripts

1. ► Audio: B-71

A: Did I ever tell you my bee story?

B: No, I don't think so. When did it happen?

A: Well, it happened when I was seven years old. I was camping with my family during the summer. While my brother and I were walking in the woods, we found a bee's nest. We started throwing stones at the nest, and then finally, I hit it.

B: What happened then?

A: Well, the bees started attacking us.

B: Were you frightened?

A: Yeah, it was scary. We started running away, and I fell down and got stung by a lot of bees.

B: How did you feel?

A: I was shocked, and I had to stay in bed for two days.

B: I'm sorry but that's funny.

2. ► Audio: B-72

A: My mom is really friendly, and she loves to talk to people. Have I ever told you some of her stories?

B: No, you haven't.

A: Well, a vacuum cleaner saleswoman came to the door. So my mom talked to her and then asked her to vacuum the whole house.

B: Did she do it?

A: Yes. She vacuumed the whole house.

B: Did your mom buy the vacuum?

A: Absolutely not. But she invited her to have dinner with us, instead.

B: She must have been surprised.

A: I think so. She enjoyed eating dinner with us, and in the end, she became a friend of my mom's.

B: That's interesting.

62

Japanese Translations

Useful Phrases

No kidding. ホントに？
Congratulations. おめでとう。
She's happy to hear that.
　　　　　　　それを聞いて彼女は喜んでいます。
Luckily, … 幸いにも、…
Fortunately, … 幸いにも、…
Unfortunately, … 残念ながら、…
before going to school 登校前に
at the time そのとき
in the end 結局、最後に
in the woods 森の中で
a bunch of flowers 花束

Nouns

event 出来事
animal park 自然動物園
school gym ［学校の］体育館
hard serve 強烈なサーブ
home run ball ホームランボール
damage 被害、損傷
cockroach ゴキブリ
bee ハチ
deer シカ
forest 森
nest 巣
pole 電柱、柱
sticker ステッカー、シール
wallet 財布
passport パスポート
vacuum cleaner 掃除機
saleswoman 女性販売員
foreigner 外国人
ketchup ケチャップ

Verbs

attack 攻撃する、襲いかかる
bite かみつく
scratch ひっかく

throw 投げる
hit ぶつかる、打つ
break a computer コンピュータを壊す
break down 壊れる
knock *something* over
　　　　　　　　　　　…をひっくり返す
get stung 刺される
bleed 出血する
stay in bed 安静にしている
run away 逃げる、走り去る
run after *someone* …を追いかける
follow あとをつける、ついてくる
come to the door 訪問してくる
come up to *something* …に近づく
walk around the town 街を散策する
give wrong directions
　　　　　　　　　　間違った道順を教える
get lost 迷子になる、道に迷う
get stuck 貼り付く、付着する
go off the road 道から外れる
come off ［靴が］脱げる
drop 落とす
look for *something* …を探す
return 返す、返却する
find out わかる、判明する
notice 気がつく
yell 怒鳴る、大声をあげる
get angry 怒る、腹を立てる
laugh at *someone* …を笑う
feel sorry for *someone*
　　　　　　　　　　…をかわいそうに思う
think of *something* …について考える
change *one's* clothes 服を着替える
vacuum the whole house
　　　　　　　　　　家中に掃除機をかける
invite *someone* to dinner
　　　　　　　　　　…を夕食に招く
become friends 仲良くなる
believe 信じる、本当だと思う
get a job as a cook
　　　　　　　　　　料理人として職に就く
give a presentation プレゼンをする

tell a story 話をする
type ［文字を］タイプで打つ
ring 鳴る
cancel 中止する

Adjectives

excited わくわくした、すごく楽しい
exciting わくわくする、すごく楽しい
surprised びっくりした、驚いた
surprising びっくりする、驚くべき
shocked ぎょっとした、衝撃を受けた
shocking ぎょっとする、衝撃的な
frightened 怖がった、おびえた
frightening 怖い、おびえさせる
scared 怖がった、おびえた
scary 怖い、おびえさせる
embarrassed 恥ずかしい
embarrassing 恥ずかしい
disappointed がっかりした
disappointing がっかりする
bored つまらない、退屈した
boring つまらない、退屈な

Adverbs and Prepositions

later あとで、後ほど
then それから、そのあと
around 周囲に
through …を通り抜けて
safely 無事に
instead 代わりに
anymore もう

Unit 12 Society

Themes: Social and world issues / Opinions
Grammar items: Asking for and giving advice
Speaking skills: Expressing opinions / Discussing issues

Building Blocks 1   Student Book: p. 86

Listen In

Answers

1. F (The woman will not go over and complain to the neighbor. She says, "That's not such a good idea.")
2. F (The woman suggests that the man talk to a teacher.)
3. T
4. T
5. F (The man suggests that the woman show her parents some documentaries about Africa.)

Audio Scripts

1. ▶ Audio: B-74

A: Jim, do you have a few minutes? I need your advice.
B: Sure. What's up?
A: Well, my neighbor always plays loud music late at night and the noise really annoys me. What should I do?
B: If I were you, I would go over and complain.
A: That's not such a good idea.
B: Then, why don't you talk to the landlord?
A: Yeah. That might work.

2. ▶ Audio: B-75

A: Hey, Cindy. I need your advice.
B: What happened?
A: I think one of the students is being bullied at school. What do you think I should do?
B: I think you should try to stop it. Why don't you complain to the students who are doing the bullying?
A: Well, I don't think that would work. I can't speak Japanese and they don't understand my English.
B: Then, how about talking to another teacher? I think it's the best way.
A: Yeah. That's a good idea.

3. ▶ Audio: B-76

A: Mark, I have a problem.
B: What's wrong?
A: Well, my boyfriend can't stop looking at his phone. He's always using some social media app.
B: That's terrible. He might have "nomophobia." You know, people feel bad when they don't have their phones.
A: Yes, that's him. What should I do?
B: If I were you, I would talk to him and tell him that he has a serious problem.
A: I already told him that, but nothing changed.
B: Then, why don't you tell his parents about it?
A: That's not such a good idea.

4. ▸ Audio: B-77

    A: Hey. Do you have a few minutes?

    B: Sure. What's up?

    A: It's about my new roommate. He always invites people over to our apartment and has loud parties on the weekends.

    B: I think you should tell him not to have parties.

    A: I did, but he never stopped.

    B: Well, if I were you, I would look for another roommate. I think that's the only solution.

    A: I guess so.

5. ▸ Audio: B-78

    A: Peter, do you have a few minutes? I need your advice.

    B: Sure.

    A: Well, I'm interested in doing some volunteer work in Africa next year, but my parents don't want me to go. They think it's too dangerous. What do you think I should do?

    B: That's a difficult question. How about showing your parents some documentaries about Africa … you know … about nature, animals, and the culture? They might understand and appreciate more about Africa if they see some videos.

    A: Hey, I think that might work. Thanks for the advice.

    B: You're welcome.

Speaking Strategy Student Book: p. 87

Speak Out

Answers

❶ good, let, agree

❷ phones, stopped, allowed

❸ feel, too

❹ think, stop, should, shouldn't

Building Blocks 2 Student Book: p. 88

Listen In

Answers

1. F (The man doesn't think that it is okay to have vending machines in school. He thinks schools shouldn't sell junk food to their students.)

2. F (Both speakers are not happy with the new highway. They mention that it is a waste of money, that there are too many roads in Japan, and that people should use public transportation more.)

3. T

4. T

5. T

6. T

7. F (The man thinks that magazines should be allowed to show any photos that are taken in public spaces.)

Audio Scripts

1. ► Audio: B-81

    A: Nowadays, I really think that schools shouldn't have vending machines selling soft drinks and sweets.

    B: I'm not sure about that. I think people should make their own decisions.

    A: Maybe, but I think it's not good. I think schools shouldn't sell junk food to their students. Do you really think it's okay?

    B: Well, I don't know. That's a difficult question.

2. ► Audio: B-82

    A: What do you think of the new highway?

    B: I think it's a waste of money. There are already too many roads and cars in Japan.

    A: I totally agree. I think people should use public transportation more.

    B: Absolutely.

3. ► Audio: B-83

    A: Nowadays, there are many young people who don't like reading. It's shocking.

    B: I agree. I think parents should read more to their children.

    A: I totally agree. Reading is so important for learning new things.

4. ► Audio: B-84

    A: I think we should ban all plastic.

    B: Really? I don't think that's right.

    A: Why? Plastic pollution is a major problem in the world.

    B: Okay. I agree, but plastic is very useful for storing food, and is very important for hospitals.

    A: Well, okay, but I definitely think we should stop single-use plastic.

    B: I totally agree with you there.

5. ► Audio: B-85

    A: I'm worried that the government is going to raise the consumption tax again. What do you think?

    B: I don't know what to say.

    A: In my opinion, it's not necessary. What does the government do with our money anyway?

    B: They build roads, pay for our health insurance and things like that.

    A: I already pay enough taxes. Personally, I think there shouldn't be any taxes.

    B: I'm not sure about that.

6. ► Audio: B-86

    A: Recently, I've been worrying about global warming.

    B: Me, too. I think deforestation is a big problem. The world is losing its forests slowly and I don't think it's good.

    A: I totally agree.

    B: In my opinion, all people should plant at least one tree in their lives.

    A: I agree. We need to stop cutting down our trees.

7. ► Audio: B-87

    A: Have you seen this magazine? It has pictures of a famous model with her friends at a hot spring.

    B: I didn't read it, but I think that's terrible. I don't think magazines should show those kinds of pictures.

    A: Why not? It's a public space.

    B: I know, but it's her private life. I really think magazines shouldn't be allowed to do that.

    A: I disagree. If a famous person is in a public place, then someone should be able to take their photos.

    B: Really?

Japanese Translations

Useful Phrases

It's a waste of money. お金の無駄です。
… and things like that …のようなこと
as soon as possible できるだけ早く
at a very young age 幼少期に
all night 一晩中、夜通し

Nouns

society 社会
human 人間、ヒト
government 政府、行政
public worker 公務員
co-worker 同僚、仕事仲間
landlord 家主、大家
owner 持ち主、飼い主
neighbor 隣人、近所の人
roommate ルームメート、同居人
private life 私生活
rule ルール、規則
culture 文化
education 教育
bullying いじめ
child abuse 児童虐待
violence 暴力
documentary ドキュメンタリー
issue 問題（点）
complaint 苦情
advice アドバイス、助言
solution 解決策
volunteer ボランティア
recycling リサイクル、再生利用
global warming 地球温暖化
rainforest 熱帯雨林
deforestation 森林伐採
fossil fuels 化石燃料
climate change 気候変動
minimum income 最低所得
vegetarianism 菜食主義
racism 人種差別
aging society 高齢化社会

endangered species 絶滅危惧種
whaling 捕鯨
environmental problem 環境問題
crow カラス
garbage （生）ごみ、残飯
trash ごみ、くず
food waste 食品ロス、食品廃棄物
disposable chopsticks 割り箸
plastic bag レジ袋、ビニール袋、ポリ袋
single-use plastic
　　　　　　　　使い捨てプラスチック製品
grocery store 食料品店
vending machine 自動販売機
soft drink 清涼飲料、ソフトドリンク
junk food ジャンクフード
competitive eating
　　　　　　　　大食い競争、早食い競争
drunk driver 飲酒運転者
cigarette smoking 喫煙
smell 匂い、臭い
air pollution 大気汚染
hybrid car ハイブリッド車
sidewalk 歩道
public transportation 公共交通機関
washing machine 洗濯機、洗浄機
electricity 電力、電気
health insurance 医療保険、健康保険

Verbs

be interested in *something*
　　　　　　　　　　…に興味がある
be worried about *something*
　　　　　　　　　　…が心配である
be angry with *someone* …に怒る
take *someone*'s photo …の写真を撮る
go to the washroom 用を足す
bark 吠える
annoy 困らせる、嫌な思いをさせる
bother 迷惑をかける、嫌な思いをさせる
bully いじめる
abuse 虐待する

harm 危害を加える、害を及ぼす
hunt 狩りをする、狩猟する
cut down 伐採する、切り倒す
reduce 減らす
destroy 破壊する
waste 無駄にする、浪費する
solve 解決する
suggest 勧める、提案する
go over （訪ねて）行く
complain 苦情を言う、文句を言う
take away 取り除く、持ち去る、連れ去る
punish 罰する、懲らしめる
ban 禁じる、禁止する
store 保管する、保存する
build 建設する
develop 成長させる、啓発する
plant 植える

Adjectives

illegal 違法の、不法の
violent 暴力シーンの多い
local 地元の

Adverbs and Prepositions

totally すべて、本当に
severely 厳しく
foolishly 愚かにも、ばかみたいに
already すでに、もう

Review for Units 10–12

Speak Out 1   Student Book: pp. 91–92

Answers

❶ so, Which, look, He's, has, Is he, athletic, he does, blonde, She's, like

❷ Did, happened, were, went, kidding, then, couldn't, in the end, Fortunately, lucky

❸ too, Nowadays, shocking, agree, think, true, totally, right, should, were, would, work

Listen In 1   Student Book: p. 94

Sample Answers

1. **a)** He is not so handsome. He's got long hair and wears round glasses.
   b) He is smart and funny.
2. **a)** She is tall.
   b) She is kind of quiet but really smart.
3. **a)** She got into a car accident. She hit a fence while backing up.
   b) Yes.
4. **a)** She was walking in the park.
   b) A dog bit her.
5. **a)** Global warming.
   b) 1. Don't buy plastic bottles of water.   2. Join an environmental group.
6. **a)** They are not good for students. They sell junk food and unhealthy drinks.
   b) No. One does. One doesn't.

Audio Scripts

1. ▶ Audio: B-88

   A: Hey, look over there. That's my English teacher. He's my favorite teacher. He's not so handsome, but he is smart and funny. I like him a lot.
   B: Which one is he?
   A: He's got long hair and wears round glasses. He's playing the guitar.
   B: Well, I hope he's my English teacher next year.
   A: You will like him.

2. ▶ Audio: B-89

   A: Who's the tall girl in the corner?
   B: Oh, that's Alice.
   A: Do you know anything about Alice?
   B: Yeah, a lot. I like her.
   A: What's she like?
   B: She's kind of quiet, but she's really smart. She was my science tutor.
   A: Really?

68

3. ▶ Audio: B-90

A: Did I tell you what happened on Sunday?
B: No.
A: Well, I went for a drive in my parents' car and I got into an accident.
B: Oh no! What happened?
A: I was backing up with the car and I hit a fence.
B: What happened in the end?
A: My parents called the insurance company. There was no big problem.
B: Do your parents still let you drive?
A: Yup. I was driving last night.

4. ▶ Audio: B-91

A: Did I ever tell you my angry dog story?
B: No, I don't think so. When did it happen?
A: Well, it happened when I was seven years old. I was camping with my family. My sister and I were walking in the park. All of a sudden, we saw a dog. I tried to touch the dog, but he got angry and bit me.
B: What happened then?
A: Well, my sister chased the dog away and we ended up going to the hospital with my parents.
B: Wow!
A: Yeah, in the end, it was okay, but I still have a scar on my arm.
B: Oh, that's too bad.

5. ▶ Audio: B-92

A: Sarah, do you have a few minutes? I need your advice.
B: Sure.
A: Well, I'm concerned about global warming and I want to do something. But I don't know where to begin.
B: Well, there's many things you can do. To begin with, I strongly suggest that you don't buy any plastic bottles of water. They're terrible for the environment.
A: Okay. I'll try that. Anything else?
B: Well, how about joining an environmental group? You can learn what to do from other people.
A: That's a good idea. Do you know any groups?
B: Yes, my friend has a hiking group that does things to protect the environment. I'll introduce you.
A: Thanks.

6. ▶ Audio: B-93

A: Did you hear that our school banned vending machines?
B: Really? No vending machines at school? Why?
A: The school thinks they are not good for students. They sell junk food and unhealthy drinks.
B: Wow. That's incredible.
A: To be honest, I totally disagree. I think they should let us make that decision. We are old enough.
B: I disagree. I think it's a great idea. Vending machines are not healthy at all.
A: Really? There are some healthy drinks.

Answers

1. **a)** T
   b) F (The man's sister is not playing the piano. She's singing with a guy who's playing the piano.)
2. **a)** F (Takako is taller than Kelly.)
   b) T
3. **a)** T
   b) F (A man yelled at the two dogs and they ran away.)
4. **a)** F (The story happened when the speaker was in high school.)
   b) T
5. **a)** F (The woman is not interested in cooking. She doesn't like cooking.)
   b) T
6. **a)** T
   b) T

Audio Scripts

1. ▶ Audio: B-94

   A: What's your sister like?
   B: Well, she's taller than me. And she's smarter than me, too.
   A: What does she look like?
   B: She's got really long hair and she's cute. Like me.
   A: Is she here?
   B: Yup. She's over there singing with the guy who's playing the piano.

2. ▶ Audio: B-95

   A: Did you know that Takako and Kelly are best friends?
   B: I know. They are very different. Takako is so tall and Kelly is …
   A: So short. Wow. She's shorter than me.
   B: And their personalities are really different, too. Takako is very outgoing.
   A: And Kelly is kind of shy. She's smart, though.
   B: Yes. Kelly is definitely smarter than Takako.

3. ▶ Audio: B-96

   A: Did I tell you about last night?
   B: No. What happened?
   A: While I was walking home from work, two dogs started following me. I started to run, but they chased me and tried to bite me.
   B: That's terrible.
   A: It was scary. They bit me on the leg but I was wearing pants, so it didn't hurt. Finally, a man saw me and yelled at the dogs, and then they ran away.
   B: You must have been so scared.

4. ▶ Audio: B-97

   A: Have I ever told you the painting story about my father?
   B: I don't think so.
   A: Well, this happened when I was in high school. My dad asked me to help him paint the house. One day, he was at the top of the ladder painting and I was at the bottom. All of a sudden, paint came down on me. My father had knocked the paint can and the paint came down all over me. I was completely white.
   B: What did you do then?
   A: Well, at first, my dad laughed so much. Then he apologized and of course, he helped get the paint off. It was actually quite funny.
   B: I wish I had been there.

5. ▶ Audio: B-98

A: Eric, I have a problem.

B: What's wrong?

A: Well, I'm not eating well and I don't like cooking. I really don't know what to do.

B: Well, there's several things you can do.

A: What do you recommend?

B: I think the best way is to get some good books about eating well and cooking. I know a few that I can recommend.

A: That might work.

B: Then, I suggest that you take a cooking class and learn how to cook properly.

A: You know, that's a great idea. Thanks.

6. ▶ Audio: B-99

A: Recently, I've been worrying about global warming.

B: Me, too. I think deforestation is a big problem. The world is losing too many trees every day and I don't think it's good at all.

A: I totally agree.

B: In my opinion, we need to stop cutting down rainforests to grow products that are not necessary. Like, palm oil, which is used for cooking and other things. Many forests are being cut down to make palm oil, but there are other products we can use.

A: I know. It's shocking. We need to save our forests. They're so important to our lives.

B: I think everyone should plant at least one tree in their life.

A: I definitely agree.

ISBN 978-4-86312-392-2
本体3000円（税込3300円）

ナショナルジオグラフィック ラーニング | センゲージ ラーニング株式会社
〒102-0073 東京都千代田区九段北1-11-11 第2フナトビル5階
Tel: 03-3511-4392　Fax: 03-3511-4391
E-mail: elt@cengagejapan.com

202102-01